FASCISM

STUDIES IN CONTEMPORARY POLITICS

Capitalism
  Economic Individualism to Today's Welfare State

Communism
  From Marx's *Manifesto* to 20th-century Reality

Fascism
  The Meaning and Experience of Reactionary Revolution

Socialism
  Its Theoretical Roots and Present-day Development

By James D. Forman

Affluent Revolutionaries
  A Portrait of the New Left

By Stephen R. Goode

Studies in Contemporary Politics offer wide-perspective examinations of major political and economic aspects of today's changing world. Using historical experience as a background, these books bring readers new understanding of the contemporary political scene.

FASCISM

The Meaning and Experience of Reactionary Revolution

James D. Forman

Franklin Watts, Inc.   New York ● 1974

Library of Congress Cataloging in Publication Data

Forman, James D
    Fascism; the meaning and experience of reactionary
revolution.

    (Studies in contemporary politics)
    Bibliography: p.
    SUMMARY: Defines fascism and discusses its origin,
its development throughout the world, and its future.
    1. Fascism—History—Juvenile literature.
[1. Fascism—History]   I. Title.
D445.F58   320.5'33   73-11480
ISBN 0-531-02648-5
ISBN 0-531-05558-2 (pbk.)

This one is for Gerdon Fahland,
an old and dear friend
who hasn't gone too far to the right,
but much too far to the west.

Contents

FASCISM

Centerville, U.S.A., 198–

The alarm radio aroused him with the usual greeting, "America, Awake!" It came to John as a cheerful reassuring sound on a day of high expectations. He arose immediately, performed thirty push-ups without breathing hard, and admired himself in the mirror. Seventeen years old, hard as nails, and not bad-looking even though he didn't make a practice of saying so.

John ate breakfast with his father, who sat behind a copy of *The People's Voice,* the only newspaper now being printed in Centerville. A few years before there had been three. His father put the paper down, saying almost wistfully, "You know, son, I canceled this thing a month ago, and it's still coming. Now I realize why." He pushed a postcard across the table; it read: "Your intention to cancel your subscription to the government paper expresses a very peculiar attitude toward our press, which is an official organ of the American party. We hope that you now realize this fact and have reconsidered. Our paper certainly deserves the support of every loyal American. Therefore, we shall continue to forward copies to you and trust you will not care to expose yourself to unfortunate consequences in the case of cancellation."

"Well?" John asked, thinking his father had made a mistake.

"Well what?"

"You still going to cancel?"

"I'd like to," his father said. "By God, I'd like to shove it down their throats, but I can't afford to. I just can't." He seemed embarrassed by John's stare. Looking at his watch, he added, "Bus'll be along, son, better eat up."

The school bus, now painted red, white, and blue so it could hardly be distinguished from a mail truck, picked him up at the corner. The day was hazy and warm, typically autumnal. Spiraling leaves fell into the old streets, which, when John was small, had been named for trees: Aspen, Birch, Cedar. They were named for generals now, and to John it seemed fitting and proper thus to honor great men.

The bus swung down the main street, named for the President. The bunting was up. Flags flew from every shop. John had helped with the decorating. He and his friends had been given the afternoon off to fix up the square with its Civil War cannon, the brass plaque for the honored dead, and the statues of Pershing and MacArthur. Only the shameful mideastern war was forgotten. They'd never have lost that one if the government had had any guts in those days.

From the small park the bus swung down lower Main and out along the river, where the mist still clung and mingled with smoke from the defense plant. The factory was working three shifts now. It had been dormant and rusting until a year ago. Hell, John thought, we can afford a little pollution. He liked the look of the billowing smoke against the light, and he'd never been much on fishing or swimming. He preferred contact sports.

Outside General Patton High the bus unloaded. In John's

FASCISM

opinion it was a good school, runner-up in the state football championship and highly rated in the recent Department of Education survey. In fact John's two complaints, an occasional misguided teacher and excessive homework, had been remedied.

The class day, in Junior B as in all other classrooms, began with the salute to the flag. "I pledge allegiance to our President and to the republic for which he stands, one nation . . ." John intoned with the others. Political theory followed with the expected weekly test and the expected questions. First question: "List the dangers inherent in the Black-Jewish-Communist conspiracy." That was easy.

John went on to the next: "Summarize the major contributions of the American party to the people of the United States." That all went back to the Near East War, which some called World War III. Most never spoke of it, for the misguided government had given support to Israel and been humiliated. The only memorial was the flying of flags at half-mast in memory of shame. Depression had followed. The United States had been without purpose or direction, riddled by poverty and rioting. Then under the President, who liked to call himself simply "the Leader," had come consolidation and new hope. All had been given work to do and a common goal, building for a proud and honorable future. John went over it point by point, ending up with "so that the United States may one day resume her proper place in the forefront of nations with new and joyous strength." That was good. It came straight from the book, and the teacher taught by the book.

Not all teachers did. For this reason, fourth-period history class was canceled. It was unquestionably for the best. John had felt uncomfortable about putting down a man that old, but as class sports leader, he had no choice. The teacher could simply have cut back on homework, and that would have ended it. John had tried patiently to explain that, in the education of useful citizens, the healthy, well-rounded body was of first importance. History, even mathematics, should be taught within a patriotic context.

"Patriotic context, always patriotic context." The old man had echoed him, adding, "And I always thought history was universal."

John had wanted to avoid a challenge, but this was asking for it. Besides, it had been brought to his attention by a fellow student that the teacher had made a joke, lampooning the leader; he had also written on a paper detailing the provocations leading to the recent police action against Cuba, *We used to call this Imperialism.*

"What about this, sir?" John had presented the paper, stabbing at the marginal note with his finger as he might at a dead snake.

"I wrote it," said the old man. "That's my opinion."

"Are you saying, sir, you don't feel the conquest was justified?"

"It's only a small island, John."

"Full of Communists, and black ones at that, spreading sedition here and everywhere else."

"Even supposing that were so, it isn't an excuse for using nuclear weapons. My God, boy, there's scarcely a living soul . . ."

"And good riddance. You're the one, sir, who's always talking about overpopulation. I don't know of a Cuban worth saving. Chile's another troublemaker."

"There simply is no justification for taking life that I know of."

"One!" said John triumphantly. "The future. The American future, worldwide. Naturally, I understand you're more concerned with the past. I'm sorry, sir, I don't think there's anything more to say."

John had brought the discussion to the attention of the supervisor, who had presented it—together with the old teacher's hesitancy in signing the special loyalty oath—to the School Board. Naturally, he'd been retired. Until a replacement was found, they exercised during the fourth period on the football field, jogging with full scouting packs. Some, including John, filled their packs with stones.

On this rousing occasion, he preferred to forget the old man. At noon the fire siren called Centerville, its workers, merchants, students, and housewives, to attention. All traffic stopped and school was over in honor of the Harvest Day festivities.

Offically it was now called the "Day of National Solidarity," and the pupils from General Patton High would march in their various contingents. The parade was led by mounted police in black uniforms, followed by a fife and drum corps, also in black. The American Girls Club followed. Clad in green, they carried American flags and motto banners: "Be Good and Noble American Girls." The scouts followed, little fellows in brown shorts and shirts. Their slogan read: "Youth Must Be Led by Youth," and it took four of them to hold it up. Next were the Young Americans. John was one of the flag bearers, out front, and he sang with the others:

> Our flag ripples ahead of us.
> Our flag brings a new age.
> Our flag takes us to eternity.
> Our flag is more than life.

John held it high: red for bloodshed for the homeland, white for the purity of national purpose, blue for the oceans and heavens to be conquered. He would die for that flag. So would they all on this first real day of thanksgiving in years. There had been no such sense of togetherness and purpose since the depression. The year before, he'd collected for the community chest and gotten almost nothing. The white feather that stood before the Post Office had never turned red. This year, thanks to the federal fund-raising drive and the posting of shirkers in *The People's Voice,* the coffers were brimming. Everyone had a job now, since the paper had printed in headlines: "Anyone who still has no job, report to the Town Hall. The battle for employment must be won." It had been won.

The parade proceeded along the main street and turned quick-stepping into Market Square. There was no disorder, though the sidewalks were thickly planted with people and flags. Last year, just before the elections, there'd been a wild time. John secretly missed the fun that had begun as the "Battle of the Bands." The American party fife and drum corps had marched as usual from the riverside into Market Square to deliver a concert of patriotic music. They'd arrived just as three truckloads of Black Fists had unloaded their own brass band in the square. The police had drawn a line down the middle and the bands had rat-tat-tatted and um-pah-pahed at each other. Their supporters had shaken placards: "For a United Greater America" . . . "Black is Beautiful" . . . "Under this sign you'll bleed, you red pig." Then somebody, no one remembered for sure who, began using a placard as a club. The picket fence on the north side of the square had quickly been stripped for weapons. Spring pipes, those nasty lead pipes loaded with a heavy spring attached to a steel ball at the end, had come out of hiding. A lot of people went to the hospital that day, and most of the Black Fists had ended up in jail.

Everything had changed since then. The Black Fists weren't only in jail now, they were strictly illegal. First there'd been the national elections. When the American party had won, most people had seemed surprised. There'd been fireworks and torchlight parades. Even before the President had been inaugurated, leftists had set a fire that had nearly destroyed the House of Representatives. At the same time, the Statue of Liberty in New York had been bombed, as had the Washington Monument, and the President had pushed emergency-decree laws through both houses of Congress, thereby amending certain sections of the Constitution and suspending civil liberties. He'd had no choice; it was that or anarchy.

With the army's support, Communists and malcontents had been arrested. In Centerville the auxiliary party police had raided the Black Fists' headquarters. Arms and explosives had been confiscated and the leaders removed to a "Compulsory Relocation Farm" ten miles upriver. There were dozens of these centers scattered in rural areas. They were receiving the black contents of the urban ghettos by the busload. Picture articles in *New Life* magazine showed what a contented adjustment the relocated slum dwellers were making, and it was certainly unfortunate, in John's opinion, that subversive troublemakers were spreading rumors about the farms. The most farfetched of these alleged that the old and unfit were being put out of their misery and subsequently canned as dog and cat food, with distribution being handled by the National Supermarket.

Apart from such nonsense, and the renaming of streets, it seemed to John that not much had changed. A couple of music societies had disbanded rather than submit to American party supervision, and the mayor, an old conservative, had been put on extended vacation. His deputy, one of the American party old guard in town, had taken over without incident. But such disturbances were all past now. The country was on the march and no further elections were planned. The President's task was simply too important.

The parade was followed by the usual speech. The principal speaker was the American party founder in Centerville. He was a war hero as well, having sunk a Russian carrier in the Mediterranean, but John's personal memory of the man went back only to the postwar days, when he was a red-nosed idler haranguing anyone who happened to pause near the statue of Patton. Now he spoke of freedom, liberty, justice, and the American way of life; of homeland, honor, mother, and sacrifice. Finally, he railed against the Treaty of Paris, which had forced massive war reparations upon the American people and un-

Centerville, U.S.A.

justly limited their military forces. Every red-blooded American regarded the treaty with shame and anger. "Clench your fists," he shouted, "and think. Never forget! Revenge will be ours!" He raised both hands in the air, a great V, the fists clenched, and many of those who listened did likewise.

Dusk was coming on when the speechmaking concluded, and John and his classmates trooped up toward the new library. The Girls Club had already set up a sandwich wagon outside, and John and the others were hungry. Everything was compliments of the party. Full darkness had come before they got down to the business on hand. They entered the library together. John was proud of the place, for it was one of the best-stocked, most modern libraries around. He especially admired the egg-shaped chairs for listening to the tapes. Once in the foyer, he took out his assigned list. The old librarian was looking at him. She didn't say anything, but she seemed to be crying silently. She made him feel uneasy, and he walked down to the fiction wing.

The books on his list were just beyond the new picture of the President, which showed him as a Minuteman on horseback, all set about with flapping flags. John began with the *F*'s; Fast, Howard. He pulled out *The Unvanquished* and *April Morning*. He couldn't help smiling. *April Morning*—that was all about the Minutemen. His father had read it aloud to him when he'd been a child. But then Fast had been as Red as you could get, no matter how well he wrote. *April Morning* fell onto the growing stack that would end as far as John was concerned with the M's. Mann, Thomas. He hadn't read any of Mann, but something must be wrong with his books when they were all on his list. Finally there was Melville's *Moby Dick*. He had wondered about that one at first, but it seemed the illustrations had been done by a Communist. With his arms full of books, he went out to the street, where the pile was growing. There were titles there he knew. *The Diary of Nat Turner,* for one, as well as all the so-called mod poets. The troop leader stood by with ten gallons of gasoline until everyone was accounted for. Then he poured it on.

When a torch was thrown onto the pile it practically exploded. Flames leaped up and the stars seemed to draw away from the rising sparks. It was a grand sight. Down in the square, the band that had been playing patriotic marches turned now to the new songs. The youths standing around the street fire began to sing along:

Dawn was breaking, sad and brown,
In the little country town,
The tramping feet went up and down—
The President's boys are marching.

To John it seemed a lovely evening. He'd always liked fires. To top it off, as the flames burned lower, the girls produced marshmallows from the sandwich wagon and they all began toasting them over the charring books. "One People, One Nation, One Leader." That was the slogan, and it seemed so true, so beautifully true. Again the distant band was playing the old tunes, and John and his schoolmates opened their mouths and sang lustily: "America! America! God shed his grace on thee, And crown thy good with victory, from sea to shining sea!" A very special day was coming to a close.

A Definition of Fascism

It is to be hoped that such an imagined day in the life of a young American Fascist as we have just pictured cannot and will not happen. There has been no demoralizing general depression in this country since the 1930s, there has been no humiliating defeat; but all of the events described in the previous chapter—and far worse—have happened in supposedly sane and civilized nations. And isolated fascist incidents have happened here. We have our Nazi party. We have upon occasions burned library books. We have fanatical thinking. Take, for example, the following, part of a mimeographed message disseminated by the White Knights of the Ku Klux Klan during the summer of 1964:

> The Communists never hesitate to murder one of their own if it will benefit the Party. . . . A case in point is the murdered Kennedy. Certainly, no President could have been a more willing tool to the Communists than was the late and unlamented "Red Jack." He cooperated with them at every turn. Yet, when it appeared to his Communist masters that his usefulness to them was at an end and that he was worth more to the Party dead

(and with his death blamed upon the South), he was callously given up for execution by those whom he had served so well. . . .[1]

It is hard to imagine more twisted, paranoid, typically fascistic reasoning, and yet even the Klan is not truly fascist. Neither are the industrialists who make warplanes and napalm, nor the university professors who research government war projects, nor the student activists who use very fascistic tactics to disrupt these projects, but they have all been called "fascist." So have the Black Panthers, who have professed a belief in violence, as the Fascists did, and whose clenched fist symbol is in fact the reincarnation of the early Fascist salute. The fact is, fascism has become an epithet to hurl at anyone or any group whose political views one wishes to discredit.

Therefore, before proceeding, a definition is necessary. Such a definition does not come easily. Fascism has no source book in the sense that Christianity has the Bible and communism Marx's *Das Kapital*. There is Hitler's *Mein Kampf* (*My Struggle*), but this is not so much a definition as a projection of what Hitler intended to do for Germany and to the world. Mussolini's *The Doctrine of Fascism,* published in 1932, was written long after fascism had been established in Italy. Insofar as fascism developed an ideology, it came as a reaction to communism and those related social themes that seemed to threaten comfortable and traditional ways of life.

The name is clear enough. It was contributed by Benito Mussolini, who dreamed of leading his nation on a quest for world power such as was achieved in the days of the ancient Roman Empire. In those days a bundle of elm or birch rods from which an ax projected was carried before Roman magistrates. Known as the *fasces,* it indicated the magistrate's power to decapitate and was a symbol of authority. It was from this word *fasces* that the term *fascism* was formed.

[1] Don Whitehead: *Attack on Terror,* page 145.

Fascism is often equated with tidy dictionary words. It has been called *dictatorship,* that is, a form of government in which absolute power is concentrated in a dictator or a small clique, usually of army officers. It has been called *authoritarianism,* which means about the same thing. These terms apply, but they do not fully cover fascism. Spain and Portugal today, together with numerous states in Latin America, can be described as authoritarian dictatorships, but they are dependent upon an army and a traditional bureaucracy without the mass support characterizing fascism. In these dictatorships, if the individual makes no political trouble, if the Church, the universities, and the businesses leave well enough alone, they in turn are left to their own devices. Fascism, on the other hand, enforces strict control on almost all aspects of life by whatever means. This is *totalitarianism,* which comes as close as any single word to characterizing fascism. And yet totalitarianism includes as well fascism's arch foe, communism.

Indeed, the two—communism and fascism—have much in common. Both have but one political party. Both subject economic life to a bureaucracy run by that one party, thereby putting an end to trade unions and genuine free enterprise. In the matter of free enterprise, communism has simply withdrawn business and industry from the private sector in most cases, while fascism encourages their profitable existence in private hands so long as they serve state objectives. Both communism and fascism narrow contacts with other peoples, socially, culturally, and economically. Both limit civil liberties to the point of extinction and apply stern censorship to political criticism.

But if they are similar in practice, they are far apart in theory and social purpose. While communism professes to be atheist, fascism clings to religion so long as religion does not put itself in conflict with the ruling power. Both call for worldwide struggle, but communism, being predemocratic and preindustrial, demands class war and the upward struggle of the worker. On the other hand, fascism, postdemocratic and postindustrial, must maintain its upper-class industrialists to support the racial war it intends to wage. In fact, one rather psychological approach to fascism has defined it simply as a fear reaction to communism.

Mussolini, who got it all under way, once described his creation as "organized concentrated authoritarian democracy on a national basis." [2] More succinctly, he called it religion. The communist Leon Trotsky was closer to the mark when he defined it as capitalist reaction. Franklin D. Roosevelt thought of fascism as ownership of the government by an individual, group, or any other controlling power, which suggests that even during the period when fascism was thriving there was much disagreement about what it represented.

To divide the problem at first into three aspects, the following questions may be asked: Who are the Fascists? How do they obtain power? And, finally, what is their objective?

Let us deal first with the identity of the Fascists. They begin with a leader gifted in verbalizing the fears of a large segment of the population. To them he is charismatic, infallible, almost divine. In every school classroom in Italy hung a portrait of il Duce, captioned "Mussolini is always right." In the case of Hitler, it was observed that the gravel upon which he had recently trod was scooped up and swallowed by his hysterical admirers. Behind the leader is a hard corps, the twenty-four-hours-a-day party members. They are his to command without question. Finally, there is a large portion of the voting public. Since fascism in general is a reaction to communism, the attraction would naturally be to those groups whose social and economic positions seem threatened by communism. This would be the conservative establishment, particularly the lower-middle class in close proximity to the Communist workers, and the industrialists and landowners whose empires might conceivably be taken over. Another group, appealed to not so much through fear as favor, is the military, for to them is as-

[2] *Opera Omnia di Benito Mussolini* (Florence, 1951), XXIX, 2.

signed the task of making the state strong among the nations of the world.

How have Fascists risen to power? Some have tried force and violence. Hitler did in 1923 and failed. Thereafter he would at least superficially adhere to acceptable political channels, as did Mussolini, but always just below the surface were terror and brute force. Enemies and potential scapegoats for economic and social ills were readily found—the Communist worker in Italy, the Communist as well as the Jew in Germany. Party recruitment was largely from the middle class, those conservative elements that felt the most immediate threat from the left. From them would come the shock troops, the storm troopers. Secondary support, more monetary than physical, would be solicited from the upper-class ranks, the prosperous landholders and industrialists to whom the threat of communism, if not so immediate, was even more spectacular.

Fortunately, considered worldwide, few Fascist groups have risen above the status of a minority party with a hysterical chip on its shoulder. Some, however, have obtained power within a national state, at which point the last democratic veneer has been rapidly abandoned. National solidarity has been asserted. Class differences have been denied and so-called misfits have been eliminated. Politically speaking, the individual has ceased to exist. The party has become the state, and the state has looked around for more enemies in order to fulfill its final objective.

That final objective, of course, is imperialistic expansion— for Italy it was a return to the Roman Empire; for Germany, the Greater Third Reich (or Empire). Initially, the goal is masked as an effort to make the state economically strong. Business, industry, agriculture are all supported and protected by tariffs and regulated in the interest of national self-sufficiency. Youth is martialed into athletic programs and schooling is narrowed, debate and criticism are eliminated, chauvinism prevails. Military forces are rapidly expanded until the nation as a whole is deemed capable of expansion. A war of conquest is the culminating goal of pure fascism. In the words of Mussolini, "War alone brings up to their highest tension all human energies and puts the stamp of nobility upon the peoples who have the courage to meet it." If a Fascist regime has survived to this point, war is provoked and undertaken with an insatiable appetite that has so far always ended in defeat.

Toward a comprehensive definition of traditional fascism then, it might be described as the seizure and control of economic, social, political, and cultural aspects of a state by a small group of activists, backed by a large segment of the conservative middle and upper classes fearful of the Communist-worker Left, to the end that the state becomes intensely nationalistic, anticommunist, militaristic, and finally imperialistic.

The Roots of Fascism

Historically, all major sociopolitical isms germinated in Europe, particularly in the four leading nations: Britain, France, Germany, and Italy. All these political systems were an outgrowth of the Industrial Revolution and the breakdown of government by monarchies. Earliest to arrive, not so much as a theory but as a natural response to rapid industrialization, was capitalism, with its individual accumulations of wealth and its private ownership of the means of production. It remains a strong if changing ism today.

In reaction to the economic abuses of capitalism, democratic socialism and communism developed side by side and still loom large in world politics. As a general rule of thumb, we may distinguish between them by noting that democratic socialism, favoring government ownership of the principal means of production, found gradual acceptance in the more advanced and industrialized nations through persuasion and the ballot box rather than by force and violence. Communism, with its revolutionary programs directed toward the same economic ends as democratic socialism, addressed itself to the bloody over-throw of capitalism everywhere, but it met with little success where the parent system was firmly planted. Unexpectedly, it did thrive in more backward, agrarian locations such as Russia and China. Yet in the chaos following World War I, it was a real threat everywhere, and from this menace fascism would draw its explosive and self-destructive strength.

When one considers fascism, one tends to picture its me-teoric rise following World War I. One usually thinks first of Germany, then of Italy, and seldom of France, but in searching out the roots of this ism one must reverse that order. France was the first to shed her hereditary kings through violent revo-lution, before the eighteenth century closed. The goal at first was constitutional monarchy, but in the fury of revolution the monarch went to the guillotine. A republican form of govern-ment never swam clear of the chaos, and though the revolution established the outward forms of democracy, the deep adjust-ments below the surface did not have adequate time to develop.

Mankind abhors insecurity as nature is said to abhor a vac-uum, so the French people, who for centuries had sweltered under the oppression of hereditary kings, chose one of their own, Napoleon Bonaparte. Napoleon, though an authoritarian and a conqueror, brought with him liberal reforms. He was no Fascist, but in two respects he prepared Europe for that era to come. He was a common soldier, risen from the ranks to be-come the popular hero on horseback, and his career became an example for future Fascist leaders of the way in which a people could be stimulated to chauvinistic fervor and conquest. Also, it was during his reign that the French aristocrats, driven into exile during the bloody revolution, began to return and reentrench themselves. They were conservatives, embittered by liberalism gone wild, and quick to react against socialistic and communistic tendencies, which would begin to crop up by mid-century.

France was to have another Napoleon, but not one like Bonaparte. It was Napoleon III who led his country into the humiliating fiasco of the Franco-Prussian War in 1870. Defeat produced a patriotic upsurge, a necessary precondition of fascism. This enthusiasm vested heavily in France's monumental efforts to build a Panama Canal. When the venture failed dismally, the French ego was again deflated and many looked around for someone to blame. A chauvinist, Paul Déroulède, with his "League of Patriots," had that someone. Long before Hitler, he accused the Jew. According to Déroulède and his new journal, *La Libre Parole,* international Jewish finance had sabotaged the canal project.

Why pick on the Jew? Irrational as it might be, it was almost a tradition among European Christians. To them the Jew was an alien with an alien religion. Assimilation was never made easy. In the Middle Ages Jews were often forced to inhabit city ghettoes and their range of employment was restricted. One occupation left open to Jews was banking and in particular moneylending. For those economically oppressed by growing capitalism the Jewish banker was seen as a usurer, a servant of the old prerevolutionary aristocracy, who was now, through financial manipulation, moving toward political power. In France the lower-middle class felt particularly threatened. However invalid these ideas might be, *La Libre Parole* accused the Jew of destroying France, and there were many people whose own interests were served by encouraging the attack.

The Panama Canal had scarcely become back-page news when the army rekindled the still smoldering embers. In 1894 an officer of the French general staff was accused and convicted of espionage for France's arch foe, Germany. The man, Alfred Dreyfus, was transported to Devil's Island and served five years imprisonment there before he was pardoned, the conviction being proved a trumped-up one. The man's exoneration made little difference. Many Frenchmen, including the French army general staff, wanted to believe in his guilt because Dreyfus was a Jew. *Action Française,* a continuing bulletin that in 1908 became a daily paper, refused to accept the acquittal. Devoted to extremist patriotism and anti-Semitism, this paper encouraged violence by young nationalists and the persecution of Jewish teachers. It went so far as to set up a club-carrying paramilitary organization calling itself "Camelots du Roi," which was a preview of the Storm Troopers to come.

The leading spirit of France's never fully maturing fascism was Charles Maurras, a young writer who hated liberalism, democracy, and the parliamentary system. In love with violence and power, he saw in the Dreyfus affair not merely an individual's trial but a questioning of his beloved army. He felt that the Jewish "Dreyfusards"—for Dreyfus had many supporters too—were out to humiliate the army and, in consequence, France herself. Paradoxically his movement was weakened by victory over Germany in World War I. The Republic had stood the test, despite his forebodings. The Great Depression of the early 1930s would briefly swell his following, but by this time Maurras' complaints seemed old-fashioned compared with Mussolini's growing success. Also, traditional French antipathy to Germany made it unthinkable for Maurras to make common cause with growing fascism in that country. Undaunted, Maurras kept up the fight into World War II. After the fall of France in 1940, a German-controlled government headed by French Marshal Henri Pétain was set up, with its capital the French resort town of Vichy. The Vichy government, to which Maurras gave his full support, was in power until 1944, when the Allies liberated France. Disillusioned, now an old man, Maurras was arrested with other leaders of this puppet government, convicted of treason, and imprisoned until 1952. Although the French counterpart of fascism never achieved power, it did introduce that form of anti-Semitic nationalism into the twentieth century just as its liberal revolution had introduced a new form of popular authoritarian leadership into the eighteenth.

Fascism came of age in Italy during the turbulent years following World War I. Like Germany, Italy had become united only late in the nineteenth century. While Germany, however, was rich and industrialized, Italy remained poor. Tempers were already cooling over the Dreyfus case in France when, in 1903, Enrico Corradini, a teacher and writer, set up a nationalistic journal, *Il Regno.* Like *Action Française,* it denounced parliamentary government, democracy, socialism, and the bourgeois society as overcautious, pacifistic, and cowardly. What it urged on the positive side was expansion and war, for it was a time when other European nations, particularly Germany and France, were building African empires.

In 1910 a new Italian Nationalist party was formed, giving political force to Corradini's ideas. Looking back to the example of ancient Rome, its supporters demanded the occupation of Libya, in Africa, once a part of the Roman Empire. About the only major difference from the French pre-Fascists was the lack of anti-Semitism. There were few Jews in Italy and there were no grounds for prejudice against them until such ideas were imported from Germany during World War II.

The Italian occupation of Libya began in 1911, and it is interesting to note that Benito Mussolini was at this time a leading light of the Italian Socialist party and editor of a party organ in Milan called *Avanti* that emphasized class, not national, struggle. So violent was his opposition to the proposed attack on Libya, an attack that years later he himself would actually initiate, that he ended up in jail. Three years later, in 1914, he was just as adamant against Italian involvement in World War I, calling it a capitalist war, but the war fever was growing. On May 24, 1915, Italy entered the fray, wisely choosing the Allied side as the one most likely to succeed.

To a far greater extent than Italy and France, Germany was a nation of vitality, strength, and militancy. Only recently built up from independent German states, the young country in 1870 found itself under the Prussian autocracy of the kaiser, or emperor. Submission to authority came easily to a politically docile people. For centuries they had been subservient to a Junker aristocracy (the wealthy Prussian landowners), the military, and a strong Church. Violent anit-Semitism had existed since the Middle Ages. The political environment, in fact, was already so strictly conservative that little room remained for the growth of a "new Right." In 1879, however, Adolf Stoecker, appealing to the lower-middle classes with his vituperative anti-Semitism, formed the Christian Social Workers' party. Already in 1883 he was proclaiming battle against the Jews until a final victory should be achieved. Riots and the burning of a synagogue in Neustettin took place. Forty years before Hitler's rise, the words "blood" and "inferior" and "superior" race were being liberally used in political speeches and university lectures. Eugen Dühring, a blind lecturer in philosophy and economics, spoke at Berlin University about the question of racial honor and the obligation to drive an inferior race from public honor.

Dühring was not the only prophet of doom. At Göttingen University Professor Paul Bötticher was suggesting a threefold program: the Germanizing of Austria, the conquest of Russia to obtain land for German farmers, and, finally, the expulsion of Jews to Palestine. He spoke of a Jewish conspiracy to dominate the world, and though he died in 1891, Bötticher's words were not forgotten by Hitler.

Even the swastika was not Hitler's invention. Theodor Fritsch, who from 1902 published a journal, *Der Hammer,* called for purity of race and popularized the symbol of the old Teutonic sun wheel, or swastika. The overabundant sense of being German, this consciousness of *volk* ("race" or "people") and of messianic racial superiority and purpose, had even earlier roots. In 1861 the poet Geibel had written a popular sentiment:

Und es mag am deutschen Wesen
Einmal noch die Welt genesen.
(Germany may one day
restore the whole world.)

There was even a ready-made "National Socialist German Workers' party" as of 1918, when the German Workers' party enlarged its title. Until that time it had been democratic in intent and tinged with an international spirit. In fact, about the only ground for Hitler to stand on in the beginning was its full-blown anti-Semitism. From this narrow base, it would not take him long to make the party over to his satisfaction.

The elements that combined to make up fascism were growing elsewhere before World War I. In Austria, the capital city of Vienna had a large Jewish population who tended to dominate the city's intellectual and commercial life. Many of these Jews were of a liberal persuasion, so that among conservatives anti-Semitism was strong. This had a formative effect upon Hitler, who was born at Braunau on Inn, a small town in central Austria, in 1889 and moved to Vienna in 1907.

Even czarist Russia, so soon to be dominated by communism, cultivated a new Right as counter to the growing Left. This group favored czar, Church, and fatherland and could put into the streets a body of young toughs. These called themselves "the Yellow Shirts" and were forerunners of the Black-, Brown-, and Blueshirts to come.

By and large, however, the pre–World War I rightists, the anti-Semites of those days, were respected teachers and politicians, not the reckless rabble-rousers who were needed for revolution. It would take the oncoming great war to shake loose the masses, destroy old values, and create the poverty, guilt, and blame upon which successful fascism feeds.

The Fascist Era in Italy

The regal structure of the nineteenth century, the world that seemed reasonable and good, at least to the fixed aristocracy of Europe, was gone. Industrialization had been gnawing at the rigid structure of society. The aristocrat at the top felt the sway, while beneath him the man of middle-class means saw the workers threatening to cut the floor out from beneath his feet. The old house was ready to fall when cataclysmic war arrived to blow it down. When the fighting was over, the Austro-Hungarian Empire lay in fragments. The Polish corridor, Danzig, the Sudetenland, Alsace-Lorraine were all unsettled territorial disputes and would all cause trouble eventually.

At the domestic level—and this included Italy as well as the other World War I victors—there was the uprootedness of increasing industrialization with its loss of identity. Most soul-destroying of all, there was inflation, which hit both victor and vanquished. Overnight, money seemed to become valueless. While farmers, in crops and livestock, owned real value, the salaried men of the lower-middle class saw their bank accounts, their life's savings wiped out. The comfortable middle class with its moderate outlook was forced to make a choice, to identify with the wealthy and conservative right, or to sink down and join the Red menace, communism.

Benito Mussolini   The early views of Benito Mussolini were not far removed from those of the Communists. As the son of an anarchist-Socialist, he had known bread riots. As a bricklayer, he had learned to hate his bosses, and he agreed with the Reds that the bourgeois world exploited the workers. From school-teaching, which gave him too small a stage, Mussolini drifted into journalism, and in 1909 he began editing the socialist paper *Il Popolo* in Trentino. It was a thorn in his patriotic flesh that Trentino, an area of the northeastern Tyrol region, which he regarded as a natural part of Italy, was then held by Austria. His flamboyant success with *Il Popolo* caused his graduation to the official Socialist paper, *Avanti.* As a Socialist, he had arrived. He was the voice of the party, but even as he rose to the top he was nearing a political parting of the ways. War fever gripped all of Europe, and Mussolini could not long tolerate socialism's neutralist stand. Presently he was out of a job, and when he set up the militant *Il Popolo d'Italia,* he was thrown out of the Socialist party.

Fasci di Combattimento   Freed of his Socialist ties, Mussolini founded "Fascia d'azione rivoluzionaria," a group to promote Italian intervention in the war. He still wanted Trentino; he was to have his war and to find it beautiful. Only the peace that followed was ugly. He saw, in 1919, the fruits of victory being swept away by a wave of communism spreading from northern Italy, and on March 23 of that year he took a fatal step. With a few dozen in attendance, mainly veteran "Arditi" shock troops, he revived his Fascia group, calling it now "Fasci di Combattimento." This occasion marked the formal inauguration of the fascist party, a relatively mild beginning, with congratulations to

FASCISM

the veterans, a denial of imperialistic goals, even an endorsement of Wilsonianism, that is, self-determination. At that time Mussolini had no doctrine in mind, but he did have the pleasure, a month later, of burning down the *Avanti* press.

All the while joblessness, labor strikes, inflation, and the fear of a Red revolution were growing. Responding to this fear, Mussolini set about organizing his groups of "Blackshirts," known as "Squadre," to terrorize and break up the leftist strikers. For the conservative landowners who saw their estates falling into Red hands, for the industrialists who pictured their empires confiscated, Mussolini was a symbol of law and order. The common enemy from below was forcing them together, and gradually the former Socialist accepted allegiance with the class he had so long despised.

The shift was made without tortuous soul-searching for, as Mussolini would later admit, "Our program is simple; we wish to govern Italy. They ask us for programs, but there are already too many. It is not programs that are wanting for the salvation of Italy, but men and willpower." Nevertheless a platform, expressed through the pages of his newspaper, was emerging, with such goals as the end of the Senate, reorganization of public transport, graduated tax, and especially a foreign policy to enable Italy to take her "proper place" among the civilized nations of the world. The result at the polls was disappointing. The Socialists did splendidly, but fascism, having not yet fully identified with the conservative Right, seemed in 1919 to have arrived at a dead end.

The identification was not long in coming. The lower-middle class, tormented by inflation, was a growing source of recruitment, while financial encouragement began to arrive from industrialists and big landowners. Even the army, traditionally conservative, well-supported, and anti-communist, favored Mussolini. In October, 1920, it gave him an official blessing when a circular was put out by the minister of war offering four-fifths of their former pay to demobilized officers who joined the Fasci di

Combattimento. The Fascist circus was growing, and it toured the country in convoys of trucks furnished by the industrialists, stopping now and then to beat up Socialists while the local police played cards. The Fascisti grew rapidly, a kind of counter-revolutionary Ku Klux Klan made up of eager middle- and upper-class youth who enjoyed terrorizing the workers—who in their turn had been knocking upper-class mothers' hats off in the streets and throwing upper-class fathers out of their first-class carriages. No distinctions were being made by the Fascisti between Socialists, Communists, and republicans; all were treated as dangerous Reds. The process, of course, was cumulative. Against Mussolini's black-shirted, tassel-capped boys, the leftists organized their own red-shirted "Arditi del Popolo" ("People's Shock Troops"). Murder and arson were daily occurrences, and by midsummer, 1922, the Socialists were driven to desperate measures. On August 1 massive strikes disrupted transportation. The government was helpless to combat the effects. Italy was paralyzed and needed a savior. Mussolini, more commonly called il Duce ("the Leader") from this time on, was not found lacking. He gave the government forty-eight hours to act, and at the expiration of that time he had his Fascists take over public transportation.

The March on Rome Suddenly Mussolini was the only force for law and order left in Italy. He began to talk of governing the country, and on October 21 proclaimed, "It is time for the arrow to leave the bow." This was a poetic reference to a proposed Fascist march on Rome. The king, imagining a hundred thousand Blackshirts slogging down the old Roman roads to the holy city, called on Mussolini to come for a visit. On October 28, 1922, the new Caesar boarded the Rome-bound express in Milan, with a last reminder to his followers to burn down the offices of the *Avanti*. They would be burnt for the fourth and last time. Caesar was on his way, and from then on the Italian railroad would run on time.

The king of Italy, Victor Emmanuel III, was a ruler in name alone. His postwar government had been characterized by inexperience and ineptitude regarding problems at home and abroad. Mussolini, who now muscled his way into the premier's chair, brought less governmental experience than his predecessor, but he was not inept and not afraid to act. In Victor Emmanuel's eyes, he seemed a defense against the Communist threat to dissolve the token remains of the monarchy. For a while Mussolini appeared to be a good thing for Italy. His initial cabinet suggested moderation to come, for only a few of its members were Fascists. The rest were traditional conservatives. The image of cool-headed, middle-of-the-road statesman was what Mussolini had in mind. He was always concerned with his image, and there was a story popular with reporters that at a very important news briefing Mussolini awaited them behind his desk, his concentration so intense upon a book that he did not even look up when flashbulbs began going off. Then one reporter, wondering about what he was reading, looked over the dictator's shoulder and saw that it was a French-English dictionary held upside down.

The moderate period did not last long. Il Duce began rearranging the electoral system so that his party—receiving the most votes—automatically received two-thirds of the seats in Parliament. Internationally, he worked on the Italian image, demanding a humiliating apology from Greece for the murder on Greek soil of an Italian general, and in 1924 coercing Yugoslavia into acknowledging that the former "free state" of Fiume (now called Rijeka) was part of Italy.

An event on June 10, 1924, hastened the process of repression. On that day a Socialist deputy, Giacomo Matteotti, disappeared after verbally assaulting il Duce in Parliament. Mussolini had closed the argument by shouting, "What you need is a charge of lead in the back." Matteotti was indeed murdered and the press attacked Mussolini for ordering the crime. His popularity fell. He sulked, called the affair a Socialist effort to discredit him, seemed guilty, indecisive, possibly on the way out. His enemies had revealed themselves, but their offensive lacked concert and concentration and began to peter out. Mussolini had been shaken but he did not fall and in the end fought back boldly, even accepting full responsibility for Matteotti's death. From this point on, he would take no chances, placate no opponents, brook no criticism. A law was rushed through giving the government power to prevent newspapers from printing false news designed to upset public order. Suppression of the press was only the beginning. Between 1925 and 1929 Mussolini became a dictator. During those years he twisted the Italian Constitution so that he obtained power to rule by decree. His Fascist party became the only party and filled all administrative and civil service posts. Those who didn't like it were beaten up, occasionally murdered, or sent on vacation to one of Italy's many Mediterranean islands, less stringent forms of what Hitler would later call concentration camps.

The Corporate State   Like most dictators, Mussolini was not satisfied with running the government. As a Fascist, he was determined to control the economy as well. The basic relevent law of April 3, 1926, established six economic sectors within which labor and capital were to be represented by national confederations of employers and employees. These economic corporations were, of course, under state control, which meant party control. This arrangement was the dream of the corporate state, an early ideal formulated by conservative thinkers to avert both communism and liberal capitalism. As Mussolini envisioned it, the Italian nation would be a living organism endowed with a single purpose, an organism that was greater than the individuals or groups of individuals that made it up. Although the scheme was more persuasive on paper than in practice, Italy did manage to weather the depression. Public work projects went forward, ports were improved, highways built, the railroads electrified. The Pontine Marshes south of Rome were drained, adding 1.5 million acres of fertile land to that available for a hungry people. By 1933 a total of 9 million acres had been reclaimed. Everyone had work. There were no strikes, for strikes were strictly forbidden. Profits were rolling in, the threat of communism was gone, and the view from the economic top seemed bright indeed. However, there were no wage increases. The worker paid for it all, an inequity about which he dared not open his mouth.

By 1929 only one powerful force was left in Italy outside the Fascist party and the old ruling class it still in part represented. That was the Church, and even here il Duce had a triumph. Since 1870 the Pope had refused to recognize the Italian government, calling himself a prisoner in the Vatican in opposition to everything that seemed tainted with liberalism, much less socialism or communism. By softening his position against the Church, Mussolini obtained the Lateran Treaties in 1929, which reestablished diplomatic relations between conservative Church and more than conservative state, making him a hero in Catholic eyes.

Il Duce had reached the height of his success and popularity. At the expense of democracy and workers' wages, especially those of workers on the land, he had brought a semblance of economic order to Italy. With domestic fascism seemingly on its feet, il Duce began to gaze beyond national borders. He liked to call the Mediterranean "Mare Nostrum" ("Our Sea"), as had the ancient Romans. Curiously, one of his early appearances as international strongman brought him into confrontation with his later senior partner, Adolf Hitler.

In 1934 he had met Hitler for the first time in Venice. Mussolini regarded Hitler as a buffoon. Hitler, on the other hand, was charmed even when criticized by il Duce for his anti-Semitism. A clash between them came later that year when Nazis murdered Austria's chancellor, Engelbert Dollfuss. Though Austria shared more ties of language and culture with Germany than with Italy, ever since his days in Trentino Mussolini had come to think of Austria as within the Italian, not the German, sphere. When the Nazis threatened to take over the country, Mussolini moved troops to the border and forced the then militarily impotent Hitler to back down and turn over the killers.

The Axis of Italy and Germany   While Mussolini had thus committed himself, Britain and France, thought of as the international policemen in Europe, had done nothing. This development came as a revelation to il Duce, who realized they were not going to stand up to Hitler. He began to picture a forceful coalition, Italy and Germany, for which he coined the word *Axis*.

By 1935 Mussolini felt Italian fascism was ready for final fulfillment—world empire. This meant war, spiritually justified within the Fascist mystique as well as economically necessary to stimulate the still-depressed economy without damaging the propertied conservative establishment. But Mussolini was cautious. At first it meant only a little war against the small African nation of Abyssinia (now Ethiopia). An attack by Abyssinians on the Italian garrison at Wal-wal was fabricated to provide provocation. The only opposition to Mussolini's retaliatory gestures were words of protest from the democratic nations of the world along with an embargo, in word only, on exports to Italy. By January of 1936 Mussolini mounted his major attack against Emperor Haile Selassie, and in four months of bombs, artillery, and mustard gas against spears and arrows, il Duce prevailed.

The victory proved more costly than expected, the territory gained of little worth, but the Pyrrhic triumph did have one consequence of world importance. The democratic nations, Italy's former allies, France, Britain, and the United States, condemned and ridiculed the modern Caesar's actions. Only Hitler smiled, and the Axis alliance was assured.

With Abyssinia barely subjugated, there came the July, 1936, revolution in Spain. At this time Spain had a republican form of government that leaned to the Left. It posed a real threat to the conservative Church, the wealthy landowners, and the business class. These elements, led by the army, began a civil war. Both Italy and Germany naturally favored this rebel side and joined cause with its General Franco, thus obtaining a testing ground for new weapons while turning the tide of battle in favor of dictatorship. Before the bloodbath was over, Mussolini had changed his views about Hitler, calling him now the "greatest statesman in the world." This change of attitude was no more clearly spotlighted than when Hitler decided to annex Austria. Four years before, Mussolini had marched troops out to resist such a threat. Faced now with the reality, he did nothing, characterizing Austria as "immaterial." Though Mussolini did not know it then, the Führer had set his hook into il Duce's broad jaw.

Germany: The Rise of National Socialism

As long as there is any recorded history of the twentieth century and any memory of fascism, they will be associated with Nazi Germany, and Nazi Germany with the one man who so single-handedly raised fascism to its brief and incredibly bloody domination in the world. On April 20, 1889, in the small Austrian town of Braunau on the river Inn, a child was born to Alois Hitler. A son and a daughter had already died in infancy. The Hapsburg emperor, Franz Joseph, still had twenty-five years to rule, but there, as surely as the hatching of a buzzard, the evil genius of fascism began to breathe and would survive. His parents named him Adolf.

Adolf Hitler Adolf Hitler always believed himself "guarded and guided by providence." He may have been lucky as far as his name was concerned. His grandmother's maiden name was Schicklgruber and Hitler's father, Alois, was born to her out of wedlock. Had not the grandfather felt subsequent pangs of conscience, married the girl, and years later adopted the son, Adolf might well have been shackled with Schickl-gruber, a name even the most stolid German would have found hard to prefix with a "Heil."

Hitler's early years form a microcosm of the discontents that led to fascism and are worth at least a passing glance. The young Hitler dreamed of being an architect or artist, and his consuming goal was to attend the Academy of Fine Arts in Vienna. How history might have been altered had he passed the entrance examinations no one can guess. Perhaps German fascism would have found itself another leader of equally insane capabilities. On the other hand, the republic might have survived the depression. It might have given way to communism. All this is speculation. Hitler failed the exams, became a casual laborer and drifter, a painter of mediocre postcards and landscapes. He might have starved to death in the years between 1909 and 1914 had he not been befriended by a Hungarian Jew, an old-clothes dealer named Neumann. Even this rare friendship was short-lived, for in Vienna Hitler was discovering anti-Semitism. The city was full of enviable Jews. The library where young Hitler could escape from the cold was full of anti-Semitic literature. During those years the Jews became the scapegoat for all his personal failures, as he would make them the scapegoat for the economic woes of millions of Germans in years to come. He arrived at other unalterable conclusions while in Vienna, namely, that life was the survival of the fittest and that struggle was the father of all things. Trust no one. Never admit defeat. Rely on the power of the will.

Hitler had moved to Munich when World War I arrived as a deliverance from frustration. He thanked heaven on bended knee for being permitted to live in such times. Without delay he enlisted in the Sixteenth Bavarian reserve infantry regiment. His later party secretary, Rudolf Hess, was a member of this outfit. As dispatch runner, Hitler had every chance of being killed in the war, for he was a fanatically brave soldier, winning the Iron Cross, both first- and second-class. Still, he rose no higher than corporal simply because his behavior was so strange. He sent no mail and received none, never asked for leave, women, or a bottle of schnapps, never cursed the war even in its darkest days. Victory meant everything to this impassioned friendless fighter, and when defeat came he blamed the international Jewish conspiracy, those pacifists, those materialists, "those vampires of Germany" whose every act was aimed at breaking down the heroic German race.

The guns were still, but there was no peace for Hitler or for many other Germans. The German Empire of the old secure days lay in ruins. Poverty, food riots, and military mutinies gripped the land. The Weimar Republic, an untried democracy, was in the hands of the Social Democratic party, which was immediately blamed for accepting the unacceptable terms of the Versailles Peace Treaty. These terms included admission of guilt for causing the war, reparations beyond the ability of an impoverished Germany to pay, and the loss of former territories.

Hitler, meanwhile, had been hospitalized at Pasewalk, his eyes weakened by mustard gas, but his will unbroken. The military had failed him, so he was resolved to try politics. Munich was a stronghold of hatred for the new Weimar Republic, and Hitler was employed by the army to investigate the meetings of Anton Drexler's newly formed German Workers' party. Hitler was immediately captivated by this anti-Semitic group, and he became the seventh member of the party committee. At this time the treasury contained seven marks, fifty pfennigs.

The Nazi Party In 1920 Hitler received his military discharge. In the same year the party's name was enlarged to National Socialist German Workers' party. Offering something for every one, the Nazi party was born. During that summer, the first "strong arm" squads came into existence. They were officially recognized the following year as the party's gymnastics and sports division, and later still as the Sturmabteilung, or

Storm Troopers, a brown-shirted imitation of Mussolini's Black-shirts.

Under Drexler, what was essentially a workers' party presented a platform of mixed planks. To the right was offered the nationalistic union of all Germans, the exclusion of Jews, and the annulment of the Versailles Treaty. To the left, the nationalization of business and the communalization of department stores was called for. But by the summer of 1921 Hitler and Drexler were engaged in a power struggle for party control. Hitler won, and he immediately threatened to resign unless he was given dictatorial party powers. The threat was a calculated risk on the part of this five-foot-eight, round-shouldered, potbellied fanatic who up to this point had been a failure in life. But this time he had gambled and won. The party presidency was offered to him and he would hold it until he died. Like Mussolini, Hitler placed power above principle, and, as his followers at this time included many members of the industrial proletariat, he paid lip service still to Drexler's socialistic planks, regarding them only as tools he would discard when no longer useful.

Once again, in 1923, Hitler would gamble. This time he lost, and the mistake was very nearly fatal. The country was on the brink of anarchy with a bankrupt government torn between the military and Junker Right and the Communist and worker Left, a situation not unlike that which had existed in Italy the year before when Mussolini threatened to march on Rome. Steadfastly an admirer of il Duce, Hitler prepared himself for a march on Berlin. Fifteen thousand Storm Troopers were put in a state of readiness. Ostensibly, Berlin controlled the army, but in Munich and the south sentiment was strong for dictatorial nationalism, and a revolt on the part of troops in that area was not impossible. Hoping to push Bavaria into an open break with Berlin, on November 8 Hitler directed the Storm Troopers to surround the Burgerbrau beer hall while Gustav von Kahr, leader of the right-wing Bavarian government, was speaking. Also present was the commander of the army in Bavaria, General Otto Von Lossow, not to mention the great hero of the recent war Field Marshal Ludendorff. Determined to pressure this group into forming a government, Hitler rushed into the captive hall shouting, "The National Revolution has begun!" He brandished a pistol in which he declared were four bullets, three for his enforced collaborators and one for himself should the putsch fail. In the confusion, only Ludendorff stood beside him, and by morning the revolution was clearly faltering.

Still depending on his own magnetism, Ludendorff convinced Hitler to march with him to Lossow's headquarters and perhaps turn the tide. With the swastika flag out front, a crowd of several thousand followed. The war ministry lay beyond a gullylike street, the Residenzstrasse, which was cordoned off by a thin, irresolute, and much outmanned line of police. At their first sputtering volley, sixteen Nazis fell dead. All the others clutched the pavement, except Ludendorff, who marched on, erect, looking to neither right or left. The police let him through. Hitler led the panic flight, alleging afterward that he had fled only so that he might carry an innocent child to safety.

This seemed to be the end for Hitler and his Nazis. Within days he was arrested, and in February, 1924, he was tried for treason. Despite his allegation that there was no such thing as treason against the traitors of 1918, he went to jail.

The Years of Preparation Politically, Hitler had made his last mistake. He had learned this important lesson: in future, he would not try to seize the government by force; he would win his way through political channels.

Hitler's sentence had been for five years. He served nine months, during which time he began writing about his political objectives under the laborious working title *Four and a Half Years of Struggle against Lies, Stupidity, and Cowardice.* His publisher had a better ear and renamed it *Mein Kampf* (*My Struggle*). In years to come, millions of copies would be sold.

Few would probably be read, although the book forecast very accurately Hitler's plans for the future: war with France, persecution of the Jews, a return to the traditions of the Teutonic Knights of medieval Prussia and to their eastern aspirations, which boiled down to the conquest of Russia.

Once out of prison, Hitler took over the Nazi party again with these fighting words: "To this struggle of ours there are only two possible issues: either the foe rolls over our bodies or we roll over theirs. And it is my wish, should I fall in the struggle, that the swastika flag be my shroud." But during his confinement the political climate had changed. Modest prosperity had returned to Germany and with it political stability, even a taste for pacifism. Hitler sensed that the times were not propitious, and he devoted the waning years of the 1920s to building up his Nazi state within a state. The Storm Trooper army grew in size and another, more ominous, black-shirted cadre was formed: Hitler's bodyguard, the Schutzstaffel or SS. Organizations were provided for the young and the old, and all the time the party was being reinforced and spreading north.

To the end of party recruitment Hitler left no stone unturned. He named enemies: the nations behind the Versailles Treaty, the Jews upon whom he blamed Marxism, defeat in war, inflation, even nudism. He used the Aryan concept of a hypothetical ethnic type descended from early Indo-Europeans. He relied on symbols, much as modern advertising does today— the imperial title the Third Reich, meaning the third empire after the Holy Roman Empire and that of Bismarck; the swastika flag; the eagles; the lightning bolts of the SS; the flashing spades of the Nazi workers' group. He used violence, strong-arm coercion in the streets against rival parties, murder when necessary.

Above all, he knew his Germans and how to appeal to the various conflicting groups. To all he pledged revenge for the Versailles Treaty and the return of territories lost in World War I that would provide the German people with the living space they needed. To the Junkers and industrialists he offered nationalism and a restoration of prosperity through war production and antilabor legislation. The middle class he would protect from the Jewish "stock exchange bandits" and from the threatened encroachment of the Communist and Socialist parties. He led the peasants to believe that big estates would be confiscated and subdivided in their interest. To the workers he pledged public education and party titles, and to the youth, whose values had been trampled and whose future seemed haphazard, he promised the world. Even so, Hitler's efforts would have fallen short and he would have been a half-forgotten quack politician of the zany 1920s had it not been for the Great Depression, which filled the world by 1930. As fortunes were lost and jobs failed, the Nazi votes began swiftly to rise. The people needed something solid to hang on to. In the midst of unstable democracy, they looked for another Bismarck, and, like Martin Luther, Hitler offered himself to them. "You are mine, and I am yours." And more and more they accepted him, a last straw in the wind, not Hitler now, but "der Führer."

Coming to Power   In the spring presidential elections of 1930 Hitler opposed the old war hero Field Marshal von Hindenburg. Though Hitler was never to defeat the old man at the polls, he would rebound from defeat saying, "The first election campaign is over, the second has begun today." He would travel by plane with the catchy slogan "Hitler over Germany." On the ground, mass flag-waving meetings were held under the cynical guidance of Joseph Goebbels, later Hitler's minister of propaganda. "The people think primitively" was Goebbels' view, and the meetings he devised were as effective and mindless as a pep rally. "What is the cause of our suffering?" would boom from the loudspeakers, and the SA (Sturmabteilung) would lead the crowd in roaring back, "The system." . . . "Who is behind the system?" . . . "The Jews." . . . "Who is Adolf

Hitler?''—and the final answer before Hitler rose to speak: ''A last hope—our Leader.'' . . .

What slogans and shouting didn't accomplish, muscles did. Until the summer of 1932, the SA had been banned from the streets. With the ban lifted, Communist parades and rallies were attacked. Many were killed, hundreds injured. Buildings went up in flames and in the July, 1932 elections the Nazis gained 230 seats in the Reichstag (Parliament), becoming the largest, though not a majority, party. The Communists, still a real threat, elected 89 members, to become their country's third-largest party. But time was running out. Hitler was already demanding the chancellorship, but Hindenburg, the aristocrat and general, denied this office to the lower-class corporal. Elections in November saw the Nazi vote cut by 2 million. The party treasury was bankrupt. The Communist party was growing rapidly and no stable government could be formed, since Hindenburg's conservatives would not unite with the Socialists, not even with the Democratic Socialists. Hindenburg tried one new chancellor after another until the only remaining possibility was Hitler. On January 30, 1933, the Hitler government was formed. A cabinet containing very few Nazis was supposed to control him. New elections were proposed for March 5. A week before, the Reichstag, the building that housed the Parliament, was gutted by fire. Officially the Communists were blamed, and Hitler took the opportunity to arrest prominent opponents— Communists, Socialists, and radicals. Opposition papers were closed down. Still, at the polls the Nazis received only 44 percent of the vote, far short of the two-thirds majority needed for control of the Reichstag.

One more step was necessary, and this was Hitler's so-called Enabling Law for removing the distress of the people and the Reich. What it amounted to was an alternative to the constitution, giving Hitler full emergency power. It required a two-thirds majority for approval. March 23 was the day of the vote.

Meanwhile, Communist deputies were arrested. Lesser parties were threatened, and only the Social Democrats had the courage to vote against the act, which was thus carried 441 votes to 94. In the streets Storm Troopers sang the "Horst Wessel Song," the official song of the Nazi party. Democracy was finished. With support from the conservative middle class and funds from the establishment, the gutter had come to power.

Consolidating the Reich Hitler, of course, was not satisfied with simple government leadership. He demanded absolute power. He now felt himself threatened by his storm troopers, a political army of Nazi adherents numbering in 1934 some 2 million strong, and particularly by Ernst Roehm, their commander. Roehm had begun calling for a second revolution. The first had destroyed the Communist and Socialist Left, and Roehm wanted to initiate another purge, this time of big business, the landlords, and the generals, all conservative forces that Hitler intended to harness to his Fascist bandwagon. Hitler needed them more in the long haul than he needed Roehm, who, with his chief lieutenants, was butchered on June 30.

Within a few days, Hindenburg, who had long held the presidency in name only, died. Thereafter Hitler simply abolished the office of president, declaring himself Führer (leader) of all Germany and demanding the army swear its oath of loyalty no longer to Germany but to him personally.

Under the Enabling Law, the Reichstag wielded nothing but a rubber stamp. Only the Nazi party survived there, and its sole function was to cheer. The civil service was quickly nationalized and nazified. All local societies, from bee-keeping clubs to kite-flying associations, fell swiftly under party control. The law courts, which so often are the last bastion of individual rights, were almost as rapidly subverted. Judges had to prove themselves politically reliable, while the actions of the swiftly growing Geheime Staatspolizei—the Gestapo secret police—were not subject to judicial review.

To curtail the expression of criticism, Hitler initiated a National Ministry of Popular Enlightenment and Propaganda headed by Dr. Joseph Goebbels, with separate departments to scrutinize radio, press, cinema, and theater. As Walther Funk said of the popular press, it was "no longer a barrel-organ from which everyone might squeeze whatever tunes he liked, but a highly sensitive and far-sounding instrument or band on which and with which only those could play who knew how, and in whose hands the Führer personally had placed the conductor's baton."

Thought control naturally reached into the school system by way of a Ministry of National Education. In the words of Robert Ley, minister of the Labor Front, "We begin with the child when he is three years old. As soon as he begins to think, he gets a little flag put in his hands." And as soon as he was able to march, he went into the Hitler Youth. By 1938 this organization contained 8 million young people, all physically fit, mindlessly devoted to their leader and their country, and all ready for war. When war came, they were rapidly conscripted into an army from which the older, more honorable generals had been largely drummed out by such means as trumped-up charges of homosexuality.

While Mussolini had come to compromise terms with the Catholic Church, granting it concessions for cooperation, Hitler wanted, as with everything else, complete state control. Hitler was an absolute materialist. For the Catholic Church's organization and power he had respect, but Germany's own Lutheran Church he regarded as cringing and contemptible. The alternative pagan revivals promoted by Nazi doctrinal fanatics were, he admitted to friends, pure nonsense, but he let them go their own way because he needed fanatics. The churches generally were starved for funds, and those rare ministers and priests who had the courage to speak out in political opposition went, with one or two exceptions, into concentration camps.

These camps for the confinement of political "undesirables" began springing up toward the end of 1933. Initially they were supervised by the Storm Troopers, whose common procedure was to ransom off the inmates to their families. In 1934 the "Death's Head" SS took over, and those who entered thereafter rarely emerged. The concentration camps were located throughout Germany, with Dachau near Munich, Buchenwald near Weimar, and Sachsenhausen near Berlin. With the coming of war and conquest came the Vernichtungslager, the extermination camps. Many of these, including Auschwitz, and Treblinka, were located in Poland.

Nazi Anti-Semitism Here, in these camps, Hitler's theory of race culminated in the liquidation during the war years of millions of Jews, not to mention countless Communists, Socialists, intellectuals, gypsies, and Jehovah's Witnesses. Though Hitler's early writings and speeches were full of anti-Semitism, the persecution had been slow to develop. Curiously, in private Hitler did not make so much of his racial theories as he did in public, saying once, "I know perfectly well that in the scientific sense there is no such thing as race. But you, as a farmer, cannot get your breeding right without a conception of race. And I, as a politician, need a conception which permits the order that has formerly existed on an historic footing to be abolished." While Hitler was a cold-blooded pragmatist, there was no end to the racial nonsense that followers who believed in his theories published, such as the fact that Jesus Christ was the first Storm Trooper, pushing over the tables of the evil Jewish moneylenders.

It was in the early thirties that German Jewry began to come under attack. Gradually, the rights of citizenship were taken from all Jews, though at this time they were still permitted to leave the country. Many did, though they were obliged to leave their worldly goods behind. More stayed, discouraged by the unreceptive mood of other lands, including the United

States. Still affected by the Great Depression, the United States was not eager to add to its "huddled masses," despite the embarrassing promises written under the Statue of Liberty. The crisis came in Germany on November 9, 1938. At the German Embassy in Paris, the third secretary had been assassinated by a Jew. This gave Dr. Goebbels the excuse for which he had been waiting. "Spontaneous demonstrations" were organized, and during the night hundreds of synagogues were burned to the ground. Hundreds of Jews were killed, but this was nothing compared to the extermination camps that came with the war.

Most notorious of the extermination camps was Auschwitz. Here the usual proceeding was barbarously simple and scientific. "Undesirables" were informed that they were to be relocated, presumably in some farming community. They were shipped in grimly overcrowded boxcars and arrived at a station that had been fixed up with a resort air. Here they were permitted to send a card home, telling how happy they were and urging relatives to follow. Thereafter came a medical inspection. Those found fit went to a barracks in the Auschwitz camp. There, sustained by a diet insufficient to maintain life indefinitely, they were worked until they too became unfit. When a prisoner was found unfit, he was discarded as dispassionately as a broken tool. While a prisoner's band played selections from *The Tales of Hoffmann,* as many as six thousand prisoners a day were stripped and sent each with a piece of soap to mass showers. (The soap was made of stone so that it could be used again and again.) Once inside, the great doors were closed and locked, and poison gas was introduced through the shower heads. In a few moments, panic, pain, life were over. The corpses were then dragged out to have all jewelry removed, along with any gold teeth, for the Berlin Pawn Exchange. Bodies were burned and the fat turned into soap for more fortunate citizens. Meanwhile, the "showers" were hosed out for the next group. In this manner Auschwitz efficiently accounted for an estimated 3 million deaths. Statistics for all the camps are beyond accurate reckoning; the brutal destruction of life beyond comparison in the history of mankind.

The Road to Conquest   Of course, the ultimate goal of any Fascist nation is conquest. Hitler never intended otherwise, but on his ascent to power Germany was militarily weak, her army having been limited to a token force by the Treaty of Versailles. There were ways around this, such as training pilots as a league for air sports and equipping agricultural tractors with armor and artillery. While this was going on, Hitler spoke of his love for peace. "Our youth constitutes our sole hope for the Future. Do you imagine that we are bringing it up only to be shot down on the battlefield?" Through the League of Nations he urged world disarmament, and when, in 1933, France refused to thus weaken herself in respect to her old foe, Hitler withdrew from the League in righteous disgust. In 1934 came the attempted putsch in Austria that Mussolini thwarted. Hitler would not be humbled again. The following year, after pointing to French rearmament, Hitler "reluctantly" announced the official rebirth of the German Army. From this stage on he would undisguisedly forge his nationalized state into a weapon.

"I go the way that Providence dictates with the assurance of a sleep walker," said Hitler in 1936. That way led to war. The first tentative step was to march German troops into the Rhineland, which had been demilitarized after the First World War. This gesture went unopposed. After all, one could argue, it was German territory. The troops stayed. Others went off to help Franco in his revolt against the Spanish government. The year 1938 was one of bloodless conquest. It began in March with Austria and the "Anschluss," a takeover of power ostensibly by local Austrian Nazis that ended with a coerced invitation to the German government to send troops to help restore order. The soldiers came, and with them were the SS and the Gestapo. Meanwhile Britain and France watched and waited, rationalizing with some merit that it was exactly what most Austrians wanted. To the great delight of the German people, who began to see Hitler as an infallible diplomat, Austria was bloodlessly incorporated into the Third Reich. One final diplomatic coup remained to him, with the occupation of a part of Czechoslovakia known as the Sudetenland, an area largely inhabited by Germans. Czechoslovakia's claim to it was questionable, and the Allies again backed away from physical opposition for the sake of "peace in our time." Only then did Hitler overstep by seizing the rest of Czechoslovakia. It was too late for Britain or France to help the Czechs, but Britain, at least, showed its intention to give no more by agreeing to defend Poland against subsequent German aggression. The stage was set for World War II.

The map and politics of Europe would be very different today if Hitler had known when to stop. That time had come, but the man and the system he had created were insatiably bent on war. Months in advance, September 1, 1939, was fixed for the attack on Poland. The Nazi "Party Rally of Peace" that had been set for August 27 was called off. At the last minute Hitler tried to obtain a peaceful agreement with Britain, allied to Poland by treaty, on the grounds that, beyond Poland, Germany had no further territorial ambitions. Britain wasn't budging this time, and when the news reached Hitler he shouted, "Idiots! Have I ever told a lie in my life?" For form's sake, in an operation designated "canned goods," some criminals were taken from prison, drugged, put into army uniforms, and shot near the Polish border. They were than produced as evidence of a Polish attack on German soil, and World War II was launched nominally as a defensive counterattack. Within less than a year that counterattack had swallowed up most of Western Europe and threatened much of the world, a world with too many aroused enemies for Germany and her Fascist allies to prevail. As naturally and inevitably as the life cycle itself, fascism had been born in domestic chaos, grown into the strong nationalized state, and gone to war. Nothing remained but the long dying.

European Fascism
through World War II

The Collapse: Italian-Style   When it came to waging war, Mussolini was basically an indecisive man. He wanted conquests. He liked to think of himself as Caesar, but he was not so unrealistic as to imagine Italy was ready for any major war. In 1937 he still feared an alliance with Germany, for as Count Ciano, Italy's foreign minister, said of Hitler, "He does not name the enemy, nor does he mention his objectives, but he wants war during the next three or four years." Before entering the "pact of steel" with Germany in 1938, Mussolini obtained Hitler's promise that there would be no major war for at least three years. He wanted to believe it, and yet, when war came the following year, he was depressed by Italian preferences for neutrality.

The German victory over France made him eager to share in the spoils, hesitant because it would make Italy seem but a "jackal among nations." He finally chose the scavenger's way and declared war on a moribund France. His subsequent military excursions against Greece and into North Africa were all disasters. Time and again German troops came to the rescue, and it was this dependency rather than defeat that doomed Italian fascism long before the war was lost. By fighting on the side of a stronger ally, the zealous Italian Fascists would naturally gravitate to that stronger power for allegiance, while the less-convinced "bourgeois Fascists" would fall back to being simply bourgeois.

Mussolini had, in effect, betrayed himself. Long before the last battle was fought, fascism was dying in Italy, and on the night of July 24, 1943, the Fascist Grand Council, which had not convened in four years, met and condemned their leader. The following evening Mussolini was discharged by the king. The party was dissolved and a new government, sponsored by the army, was formed with the objective of surrendering to the Allies. They did not act quickly enough. German troops occupied the country and il Duce was put at the head of the puppet state. He would hold this humiliating post for the better part of two years, years that would turn his country into a wasteland. His personal agony would come to an end before a partisan firing squad on April 28, 1945. For this last of the Caesars and first of the Fascists, the only remembrance would be as follows: "Si monumentum requiris, circumspice." ("If you seek a monument to him, then look about you.") Italian fascism lay in ruins.

The Collapse of National Socialism   "Poor, poor Adolf, deserted by all, betrayed by everyone. Better that ten thousand others perish than that he be lost to Germany." Thus Hitler's former mistress and last-minute bride, Eva Braun, would lament on the very day that Mussolini died. Hitler would survive his partner in crime by only two days, becoming a suicide on the afternoon of April 30, 1945, but his national socialism had remained fanatically intact until his death. Most Germans concurred with Eva. As long as Hitler lived, there was hope, and instead of going into decline when the war became difficult, as was the case with Italian fascism, the Nazi party tightened its hold upon the nation, while Hitler secured his personal grip not so much upon the party as upon the army.

By the time the great 1941 offensive was launched against Russia, an attack that Hitler had predicted nearly twenty years before in *Mein Kampf,* he had almost totally lost interest in Germany's domestic affairs. The war absorbed him, and on December 19 he took his last megalomaniacal step by declaring himself the active commander and chief in the field. Hitler was the consummate political manipulator, but his attempt to impose these gifts on the grand strategies of global war only hastened disaster. Against the advice of his more talented generals, he divided his forces in Russia. Never would he sanction withdrawal, and his policy of holding every inch of ground, regardless of the cost, made the defeats that much more terrible when they came in North Africa and at Stalingrad in Russia in early 1943.

Incapable of assuming the blame himself, Hitler accused his field commanders. He dismissed many, replacing them with yes-men and Nazi fanatics, a tendency that he greatly accelerated after an assassination attempt on him on July 20, 1944, put into effect by a group of regular army officers who wished thereby to end a hopeless war. With these men and their civilian confederates rounded up and for the most part executed, there was no effective resistance left in Germany. The party, led by men for whom defeat could mean only humiliation and death, was prepared to fight to the last German. The rapid final collapse, the failure of communications, and a natural human desire to survive made this impossible, but Hitler's ideas never changed to the end. On April 29, 1945, in his last political testament, he would write: "It is not so that I, or any other German, wanted war in 1939. It was wanted and begun only by those international statesmen who either were of Jewish ancestry or served Jewish interests."

Hitler's Far Eastern Partner: Japan Japan, a severely overpopulated island nation, was the third vital member of Hitler's Axis. The Japanese leadership shared Hitler's dream of broad conquest. They hoped to dominate China and the Pacific area, and they promoted the same flag-waving chauvinistic crowds. They were called Fascists, but they were Fascists in the same sense that they were honorary Aryans, for, if the surface texture resembled European fascism, the ingredients were a far different blend.

Until 1853, when Commodore Matthew Perry visited Japan, that island nation lived in virtual isolation from the commerce and ideas of the West. It was a land ruled by old Warrior lords, the shoguns, where the emperor was a god. The emperor would retain his divine cult through World War II, but in other respects the impact from the West was rapid and profound. The Japanese had an astonishing capacity for imitation, not only industrially but even politically. In the 1920s Japan was experimenting with democracy, but, of all the lessons learned, the one taken closest to heart was that of Western imperialism.

Toward the end of the nineteenth century Japan's first objective was to become the equal of the West. Initially the focus was largely inward. In 1889 constitutional government was inaugurated under the Meiji Constitution, with policy placed in the hands of a group of elder statesmen who advised the emperor. Between 1912 and 1926 the emperor was mentally deranged, and a growing bureaucratic leadership took over. Massive industry kept pace and, with it, the usual population explosion. Within sixty years the population more than doubled. Food had to be imported. While Germany found a scapegoat for her troubles in the Jew, the Japanese, with some validity, pointed to Western discrimination against orientals. Australia, where job opportunities were plentiful, barred Japanese immigration entirely. The United States made entry almost as hard, and Japan began to echo the German call for living space.

Fascism in both Italy and Germany had come about as the result of the conservative middle and upper classes overreacting to the postindustrial growth of a working-class communism, with the army tagging along for the glory. Fascism, Japanese style, was more directly a military matter. Like Prussia with its proud military caste, Japan had its selfless Samurai tradition, which looked down on grasping politicians and vacillating government. Various societies grew up among the younger officers, such as the National Purity Society. The objective was to purge Japan of Western liberalism and return the nation to the military virtues of older days. When the time came, it would be these young warriors who would entice the politicians into war, and not the reverse, as was the case in Germany.

By and large, the Japanese junior officers avoided political activity. Their inclinations, of course, were conservative. A few were professed National Socialists. The leader of this faction was Ikki Kita (1883–1937) who wrote *Outline Plan for the Reconstruction of Japan,* in which he advised setting aside the constitution for a revolutionary regime headed by a military government that would nationalize most property, limit individual wealth, and take over Asia.

In order to push the army and its older generals into national leadership, a number of terrorist groups sprang up in the early 1930s. Their objective was to seed turmoil and embarrass the government, thereby obliging the army to step in. They were very nearly successful. In 1932 the prime minister, Tsuyoshi Inukai, was assassinated. Many political murders followed, and in 1936 one revolt led by junior officers took control of Tokyo. This was going too far, and the leaders were rounded up and executed, among them Ikki Kita.

Despite purges of the more extreme elements, the new militarism was growing in influence. Its leaders looked to the throne, where Emperor Hirohito had taken over in 1926 from his mad predecessor. Gradually the moderate balance was eroded away by that chauvinistic process which occurs in every modern country preparing itself emotionally for war. Aggression, in Japan's case the gradual encroachment upon Manchuria, led to international criticism. Criticism, particularly in a land sensitive to foreign discrimination, increased patriotism and gave further support to the generals.

In 1937 parliamentary government remained popular with the people, as did their weak prime minister, Fumimaro Konoye. By this time military involvement in China was approaching the status of a major war, and the following year the Konoye government pushed through a national mobilization law that gave it sweeping political and economic power to deal with the emergency. Still, the institutional structure of the Meiji Constitution was never altered, nor did the wartime government achieve complete control over the military. The emperor remained a nominal god and the traditional familism, which formed the backbone for economic strength, never gave way to the modern totalitarian state.

When he failed to negotiate successfully with the United States in 1941, Prime Minister Konoye resigned. His war minister, General Hideki Tojo, succeeded to the post. The United States continued to insist that Japan withdraw from Indochina, which it had invaded. Japan had no such intention and ended the discussion by attacking the United States Naval base at Pearl Harbor on December 7, 1941. A rush of early victories followed, and General Tojo began to imitate the behavior of his Fascist allies. His dominance, however, was never that of Mussolini, let alone Hitler, for this was not political fascism in which a conservative civilian population had participated heart and soul but rather militarism given fair-weather support by the rest of society.

When the war started to go badly, Tojo was out of a job. Kuniaki Koiso took over and formed a war-direction council. Unlike the politicians in Germany, these men had no illusions about Japan's chance of winning the war, but, also unlike Germany, they were up against a determined military. Even into

1945 the generals continued to hold out for prolonging the war, although at the same time the emperor was meeting with senior statesmen on whether to capitulate. In April, with Germany and Italy in ruins, Japan's vacillating government fell, and a new premier, Admiral Kantaro Suzuki, took over. His problem was not whether, but how, to end the war. Military extremists held out to the bitter end, even after Hiroshima and Nagasaki had been demolished by atomic bombs, but failed in their last-ditch effort to block the emperor's radio announcement of surrender in August of 1945.

Japanese militarism with its Fascist aspects was immediately swept away with the postwar occupation by the United States Army. Governmental reforms were instituted. The older constitution, which placed sovereignty in the imperial institution, was reformed so that power would derive from the will of the people. The emperor, who proved to be favorable to democratic change, opposed conservative foot-dragging and accepted his own demotion from god to a symbol of the state. The militaristic Right was purged, General Tojo was tried as a war criminal and hung, and Japan has moved ahead into the postwar world as an example of successful capitalistic democracy.

Spain   Spain under General Franco has often been characterized as Fascist. It has long been a country prone to political experiment, and, during the unsettled years between the two great wars, a rainbow spectrum of political parties existed and were active there. At the extreme Left there was the anarchist group, disavowing central government in any form, then the Communists, Socialists, Republicans, Monarchists, and finally, at the extreme Right, the Falangists. The latter group, their name deriving from the Spanish word for phalanx, were avowed Fascists.

Since the days of its Renaissance glory, Spain had withdrawn into a backwater, dominated by a powerful Catholic Church and a do-nothing nobility. The peasants were poor and helpless, but, with the late flowering of industry, a strong working class had begun to emerge in the 1920s, led politically by leftist syndicalists who dominated the trade unions. Here was the inevitable provocation from below, and the conservative upper and middle classes watched this leftist growth with distrust.

Finally they called on General Miguel Primo de Rivera to form a government. What the general brought with him in 1923 was a strict military dictatorship. For a political program he offered only patriotism, the union of all Spaniards regardless of political persuasion, and an end to representative party government. This, as far as it went, pruned back the threat from the Left.

With the general's illness and death there came a brief revival of republican strength. General elections were called for 1931, and they resulted in a sweeping popular victory for the Republican Socialist party. With this so-called Second Republic, the moderate middle ground between radical Left and Right had come to the front. Prospects were hopeful of moderate government to come. King Alfonso, who had occupied the throne quietly under Rivera, packed his things and left Madrid forever, becoming the only Bourbon to surrender his crown without bloodshed, though the Carlists, his political adherents, have called ever since for the return of a member of his line to the throne.

The bloodletting would come soon enough, for the government kept only a wavering balance between the polarizing forces of Left and Right. Needless to say, the rich, made up primarily of the landowners, Madrid bankers, and the Church, all with the support of the army, felt themselves threatened from the Left. This fear lead to fascistic reaction.

In 1931 two young students, Ramiro Ledesma Ramos and Onésimo Redondo Ortega, who had spent some time in German universities where they had met National Socialists, began publishing a weekly, *The Conquest of the State*. This paper demanded a militarized state and called for the nationalization of key industries. The same year, these two formed Spain's first Fascist party, "Juntas de Ofensiva Nacional Sindicalista" ("Groups of National Syndicalist Offensive"). At the international level, they urged the acquisition of Gibraltar, Morocco, and Algeria.

In 1933 a second Fascist party was founded by General Primo de Rivera's son, José Antonio Primo de Rivera. He called this group the Falange Española, and it quickly absorbed the earlier party. With aid from aristocratic financing, the Falange grew swiftly. Its symbol was the yoke and arrows, a blue-shirted uniform, and the Fascist salute. Superficially it followed the Italian-German pattern. In other respects it differed. Rivera was an aristocrat and scholar, and he had no such rapport with street fighters as had Hitler and Mussolini. In fact, it has been said of him that he conceived of fascism as simply an intermediate step from which in time a more communistic form of government would peacefully emerge.

Meanwhile the Second Republic was in trouble. A revolt by the Asturian miners (strong communists) had pushed the government, already battered by the political Left and Right, toward the conservative side. Against this tendency, a leftist coalition of Communists, Socialists, Syndicalists, and Republicans contrived to win decisively at the polls in 1936. Their union was discordant at best, and their success immediately opposed by the Church, the army, landowners, industrialists, and monarchists. As spring turned to summer, political tension mounted. The Falange was ordered dissolved by the new government. Rivera went to jail, from where he warned his party not to combine with the army or the traditional Right. His advice went unheeded. That summer came the revolt of the generals, and the leaderless Falange set up a militia in their support. Ironically, in November, Rivera was tried and shot by the republic for initiating this revolt, which he saw as a disaster to his cause.

The revolt of the generals had been planned as a quick,

relatively bloodless takeover of key positions, but within forty-eight hours of the revolution's outbreak, all political institutions had collapsed. The Spanish state had died, and a chaos of armed minorities ensued, with such orders going out as "Spare the velvet trousers [the peasants]" and "Shoot all the blue overalls [the workers]". Not until October 1, 1936, was Franco elected chief of state for the rebel side.

The Spanish Civil War Taking the side of the duly elected republican government were the workers and peasants, anarchists, Communists, Socialists—a whole spectrum of diverse occupational and political-interest groups. They were ill-armed and poorly led. Although they had the popular sympathies of the Western democracies, they were denied official aid. Volunteer groups such as the American Abraham Lincoln Brigade were formed, but their only extensive help from outside was from the Soviet Union. This aid came at a price, for it was given not to Republican Spain but to the Communists within Republican ranks, and their interests often diverged, creating a near civil war within the greater civil war. Meanwhile Franco had the traditionally conservative elements behind him, which meant trained soldiers and financial backing from the business and landed community. He solidified his position and began to close in upon the republic, whose defensive perimeter took in the major cities of Madrid and Barcelona. For two bloody years the issue hung in the balance, while massive help arrived from Fascist Italy and Germany to break the stalemate in Franco's favor. In 1938 Barcelona fell as Republican refugees fled on foot through the snowy Pyrenees mountains to France. In Madrid the hard core of Communists would have fought on, but for international communism, not for the Spanish Republic. With the capture of Madrid on March 28, 1939, the Spanish civil war was over. World War II was about to begin.

Germany was, of course, interested in the possibility of a Fascist ally and so did what it could to build up the revived Falange. General Franco also accepted the Falange as an ally at first. The new Fascist leader was Manuel Hedilla, whose brand of national socialism was mistrusted by Spanish conservatives, as was his conspicuous link with Hitler. In the end, Franco had him arrested, knowing that Hitler would not chance splitting up the rebellion by supporting the Falange in opposition. With Hedilla in jail, Franco decreed a fusion of the Falangists and the Requetés (the name chosen by Spanish monarchists). These factions had no common bond whatever except Franco's personal leadership. With the army to ensure his position, this was just what Franco wanted. From then on, he allowed himself to be called el Caudillo, "the Chief," and so he was in very fact, with the Falange as helpless as Rivera had feared. Its last real hopes of assuming political dominance in Spain perished with victory over the Left, for the victory belonged to the military dictator, his army, and the conservative coalition that gave it support. The Falange had failed to become indispensable. Conservatism had managed, without fascism, to put down the Left, and German assistance, which, whenever possible, had shown itself partial to the Falange, came to an end.

Other Incidents of European Fascism   The period between the two world wars was the age of fascism throughout Europe. The growth of nineteenth-century capitalism had prepared the soil. It had added big industrialists to the traditional landholding elite, and it had created the working class. The workers were voiceless at first, but in time they would demand their economic and political rights. Then the conservatives would stiffen in resistance, knowing those rights would come at their expense. Between Left and Right, the middle class was a buffer, and it felt the squeeze when the tension between opposing sides became dangerous, augmented by war damage, economic inflation, or depression. From middle-class ranks that feared they were being submerged would emerge the Fascists, ready to serve the establishment as shock troops for what they considered a good and traditional way of life. Of course, in each of the three groups there were variables, strengths and weaknesses that made for a spectrum of results. In some cases the Left prevailed, most notably in the Soviet Union. In others, as in Spain, the traditional conservatives overcame the threat from below with only subservient support from fascism. Finally, as in Austria, there was the case of fascism prevailing only when it received help from outside.

Austria had been Germany's ally in World War I and had remained close to Germany economically, philosophically, socially, and in its desire to return to the strong leadership that had been lost through defeat. Austria had been greatly reduced in size by World War I with the breaking down of the Austro-Hungarian Empire. It had the poverty and confusion of purpose upon which fascism must feed, and it had the Communist threat, particularly in its capital, which was referred to in those times as Red Vienna. Many of these Communists were of Jewish ancestry, which filled in all the requisite conditions of prejudice and hatred.

Though the Austrian Army had been shattered by the war and the terms of the peace, many paramilitary organizations survived. Calling themselves "Heimwehren" (Home Defense Units) their goals were anti-Marxist and antiparliamentarian. In general they favored a corporate economy under which labor was controlled and industry guided by the state. This pattern was in keeping with fascism, but they were held back during the 1920s by discord among the various Heimwehr leaders. The competition continued into the 1930s, by which time Hitler had risen to power, and a great part of the Heimwehr crowd began gravitating into the National Socialist party. Surviving elements of the older Heimwehr continued to derive support from Mussolini, but this support diminished as Hitler's influence grew. In the end, of course, National Socialism triumphed. Its Austrian membership paved the way for the 1938 Anschluss, which in effect was not a triumph for Austrian fascism, but for German imperialism. From this point until it was occupied by the Allies at the end of World War II Austria remained a German puppet and a second-class citizen of the Third Reich.

In general, the smaller countries of eastern Europe were more receptive to fascism than were the nations of Scandinavia or western Europe, where democracy had a tradition of natural growth and where a government representing the middle ground could peacefully moderate between emergent Left and threatened Right. Unless one insists on characterizing the Metaxas regime in Greece as Fascist, these eastern European Fascist parties never achieved power. They served the regime, as the Spanish Falange had served General Franco, and national leadership tended to be drawn from the military or the conservative establishment, not from the Fascist street fighters of the middle class as with Hitler and Mussolini.

Finland was typical. On the one hand were close ties with Germany, on the other the threat of Soviet communism. Its soldiers returning from the First World War brought with them the hope of a Greater Finland, and in 1922 they formed the "Academic Karelia Society," whose formal salutation was "Brothers in the Hatred of Russians." Russia was the enemy rather than the Jews. Another overlapping group called itself the "Lapua Movement," and it demanded first, the legal elimination of the Communist party, and second, the end of parliament itself. This movement, which had begun as expansionistic and anticommunist, gradually became more authoritarian and fascist-oriented as Italian and German influence grew. Failing to gain sufficient support at the polls, the Lapuans attempted to seize power by force in 1932, but the revolt was crushed. Fascist influence, however, continued to grow from without as Germany and Finland made common cause against Soviet Russia. In the winter of 1939–40 the Red Army attacked Finland and gained territory. In 1941 Finland cooperated in the German attack on Russia, seized back the lost territory, and gained some in addition. Three years later these territorial gains were lost once more, but Finland never surrendered her political integrity, giving way neither to National Socialism nor to Soviet Communism.

National Socialism had better success in Hungary. After World War I that country experienced civil war, a brief Communist regime, and a counterrevolutionary "white terror," which saw Communists hung and Jews murdered. As the Communist leaders were mostly Jewish, traditional anti-Semitism became more violent. The government that emerged from this civil strife was conservative, nearly feudal, and partial to the far Right. Its minister of defense was one Julius Gömbös, an anti-Semitic nationalist who, in 1923, founded the "Party of Racial Defense." Styling himself after Mussolini, he finally became prime minister. His objective was a one-party fascistic system, but he lacked unity of support and died in 1936 without achieving his ends. The problem in Hungary was not too little fascism, but too much. The competing groups, many of them verging on the lunatic, simply couldn't get together. One group developed a new mystical creed of Turanians, worshiping a warlord called Hadúr, the ancient Magyar god. Another assortment, calling itself the Arrow Cross, followed Ferenez Szálasi. This man believed God had selected him to redeem the Magyar people and felt, as Hitler did, that providence had put a special force inside him to accomplish his objectives. Szálasi went to prison in 1938 for writing subversive literature. There his popularity grew. With the coming of war the old ruling class continued to govern. Since the Arrow Cross was suspected of serving German interests, it was kept in check throughout most of the war. Only toward the end would Szálasi have a moment of tainted glory. Fearing that a valuable ally would presently fall to the Soviet Army, Germany took political control of Hungary, with Szálasi as nominal head of state. By this time, however, Russian troops were already on Hungarian soil and the days of Szálasi's career and Hungarian fascism were numbered.

Rumania was another eastern European country that flirted

with bizarre forms of fascism between the two world wars. She had gained territory in the first, and along with the land had come an enlarged Jewish population and extreme anti-Semitism. Reminiscent of the Ku Klux Klan was the "Legion of Archangel Michael" whose membership fancied themselves crusading knights. They rode through the countryside inciting the peasants "in the name of the cross" to fight "Godless Jewish powers." This group had an elitist character and attracted no large following, but in 1930, to attract the crowd, the Garda de Fier ("Iron Guard") was founded to resist Jewish communism. The Iron Guard rapidly gained strength. Opposed to it was King Carol, a rightist who sympathized with Germany. Under Carol, the Iron Guard was mercilessly persecuted both legally and illegally, and many of its leaders were garroted while supposedly attempting escape. Later, when the king was exiled and the army took over the government, the Iron Guard once more gathered itself, but in a final trial of strength the army prevailed.

Greece is called the cradle of democracy. After World War I and its own war with Turkey, Greece seemed about to honor this birthright by settling down in 1924 to a republican form of government. It lasted only a year. Then General Theodoros Pangalos usurped governmental power, only to give way within a year to General Georgios Kondyles. One government followed another in monotonous succession until the return of King George II in 1935. The next year, with the king's consent, General Joannes Metaxas became premier in name and dictator in fact in order to forestall an alleged Communist coup. His regime, which he called "the Third Hellenic Civilization," reminiscent of the "Third German Reich," has been called fascist. It used the Spartan salute and it officially emulated the virility of that stalwart people. Communism was its arch foe; Metaxas was a typical military dictator. He was not unpopular, but he did not achieve power through massive political support. Though anti-communist, he was not anti-Semitic, and he made no advance toward the corporate society. If he had territorial ambitions and a Fascist's lust for war, he was given no chance to exploit the former or initiate the latter, for in the fall of 1940 war was thrust upon him by Italy. This unprovoked attack was successfully resisted by Greece, but by the following spring Metaxas was dead, his successor a suicide, and the king in exile. The Germans took over from their incompetent ally and swept through Greece in a matter of days. Greece lay under alien Fascist dominion until 1944, when it was liberated. Since that time the usual unstable governments have shifted, Left, Right, and center. The power is presently in the hands of the army, a military dictatorship once more, but not in the true sense Fascist.

Before leaving fascism in eastern Europe for the west, one final country should be mentioned. This is Soviet Russia, where communism has flourished. It took wealth and power from the middle and upper classes and put it into the hands of a workers' government, the dread of all professed fascists. However hostile economically, the two systems had common ancestry, sharing the fall of monarchies, the discontent with raw capitalism, and the parliamentary system of government as a setting. With the ascendancy of Joseph Stalin in Russia, the gap narrowed and a number of Fascist traits appeared within the Soviet system. There was the cult of the one and only leader, Stalin, whose name means "Man of Steel." There was the narrowing of power into dictatorial hands, the glorification of the past, the purging of old party members, and the growth of concentration camps. There were even territorial ambitions. These were all Fascist elements, which have diminished since World War II and the death of Stalin.

Western Europe to a lesser extent flirted with fascism. France, which as much as any country gave it an intellectual start, has already been discussed. Belgium is a country divided between the French-leaning Walloons and the Dutch-leaning Flemings. The more radical elements of the latter population had long favored a separate kingdom of Flanders, which would be strongly tied to Germany. In 1933 the Vlaamsch National

Verbond was formed. Its members were anti-Semitic and anti-capitalist, wore party uniforms, and waved flags, all in imitation of their German brothers. Their very pro-Germanness isolated them from the bulk of a basically patriotic population and so they remained a minority up until World War II, when Belgium was overrun by Germany.

Fascism's most steadfast foe from first to last has been Great Britain. Nevertheless, always tolerant, always entertained by eccentrics, Britain had her Fascists, too. Most were disillusioned middle- and upper-class conservatives who wanted to preserve the fading empire or the purity of the English race. One group, organized by Arnold Spencer Leese, called itself the "Imperial Fascist League," wore black shirts, flew the Union Jack with a black swastika in the center, and channeled their hatred toward the Jews.

The largest Fascist group in Great Britain was a product of the economic depression. Its founder, Sir Oswald Mosley, went to Italy to study Fascism in 1932. When he returned, he instituted his own corps of fascist-saluting Blackshirts, who spent most of their time guarding his headquarters, a "Black House" in Chelsea. Mosley had a taste for trumpet fanfares and finely staged meetings. His main theme was anti-Semitism, and he characterized the Jews as a nation within a nation with allegiance other than to Great Britain. Mosley had the makings of a talented Fascist, but he arrived too late in a land where democratic government had largely moderated the economic inequities between political Left and Right. His main theme, anticommunism, was a dull issue in a country where few Communists existed. Besides, his efforts were tainted by his obvious attachment to Hitler. A mass following never developed and, with the war's onset, Mosley and his hard core of Blackshirts were bundled off to jail and postwar obscurity as an activist in the black-white confrontation.

As the war ended fascism in Britain, so it would sooner or later in all other involved countries. Even if left to their own devices, the defeated nations would undoubtedly have come up with altered governments thereafter, but no such probability was left to chance. In the sphere of their influence, the Western Allies as much as possible insisted on democratic forms, while the Soviet Union implanted subservient communism in the East. Only in certain countries uninvolved in World War II would significant fascism, or its related forms, survive, and the latter part of this book will be devoted to their study. First, however, there will be a consideration of the system's economic side, for despite the hysterical speechmaking, the rioting crowds and the inevitable thunder of guns with which fascism is associated, it is basically a reaction by conservative capitalism to alternatives proposed by communism and socialism.

The Economic Structure of Fascism

As has been mentioned before, several sociopolitical isms have developed in response to the industrial age. Capitalism is the result of individual industrialization, while both communism and socialism are responses to capitalism and an attempt to curb it. All of these systems are basically different economic theories at work. Under democratic capitalism, the society is thought to function best if the individual and his money are given free reign, a theory modified in recent years by growing taxation, controls on monopoly, and other such limitations on individual economic freedom. As unbridled capitalism tended, particularly in the nineteenth century, to exploit and degrade the worker, communism and socialism arose as champions of the worker's cause. The former took a violent revolutionary and totalitarian shape, while the latter clung to the democratic forms of Western civilization such as free elections and majority rule. All three systems continue to exist in competition today. Fascism was a latecomer. It could not have been otherwise, as it needed the fear of full-grown communism to give it impetus. Its successful leaders, by and large, were men of the lower-middle class, spokesmen of that conservative group which felt its traditions most directly imperiled from below. At best, economics was to them an unpleasant necessity, but money was vital to a war economy. An alternative program to that of communism was unavoidable, so fascism's various practitioners fabricated theories that, for want of a better catchall term, might be called "state capitalism." This state capitalism had as its final objective a nation geared for war, which meant regimentation and subservience to the state from top to bottom. The big capitalist was given support as long as he in turn supported the system, and the worker was deprived of collective power. It remained only for the fascist leaders of Italy, Germany, and Japan to structure their individual systems.

Italy Mussolini's prime concern was thwarting communism and gaining political power. He wanted to run Italy, and at first he didn't much care how. Once his goal of attaining political power was achieved, he set about forming a policy of economic protectivism, which would neutralize the worker below and isolate domestic industry from foreign competition. The objective was the corporate state. As Mussolini projected it on paper, its chief ingredients were five: (1) state control of foreign trade, wages, and prices; (2) prohibition of free collective bargaining and trade unions; (3) no free private enterprise; (4) subsidizing of large-scale enterprises by the state; and finally (5) establishment of industry-wide corporations with obligatory membership for all formerly free businesses.

Such rigid economic control had historical precedent in the old merchant guilds of Genoa, Florence, and Venice, but the new system was slow in getting started. Until firmly established, Mussolini needed the backing of the big landowners as well as of private businessmen who, in their fear of communistic takeover, had largely financed his black-shirted army during the street-brawling days. Another difficulty was with industry itself.

Fascism needed big industry for war production, and Italy was primarily agricultural, having little industry and even less of the basic raw materials that make it run. Without domestically available metals or basic fuels, Italy, like Japan, lacked from the start the self-sufficiency vital to a militant Fascist state.

Twelve years had passed since the Fascist seizure of power before steps were taken to develop actively the corporate state. And then they were initiated only under the impetus of world depression. In 1932 Mussolini set up the Ministry of Corporations. All persons of similar occupation or trade were to be grouped into a single syndicate, with the various syndicates being centralized into provincial unions and further into national category federations. All-inclusive parallel employee organizations were to be grouped into a pseudomilitary hierarchy of national federations, confederations of federations, and at the top a national council of corporations. The groundwork had been set up in 1926, but not until 1934 were the category corporations established. Heading up this corporate army was the Ministry of Corporations, the Central Corporate Committee, and the National Council of Corporations. What it all amounted to in practice was an enslavement of the workingman and the suppression of his union strength with its tendency toward communism and higher wages. At the capitalist level, the system leaned toward big business combinations under government control. Voluntary mergers are a natural capitalist tendency, but Italy moved toward compulsory cartelization. The installation of new factories as of 1932 was made subject to government license, with big businesses being favored over small. Basic industries such as cement, steel, and construction were put to work initially on massive public works programs: port improvement, highway construction, the electrification of railroads. Toward the self-sufficient "fortress economy" to which all Fascist nations aspired, a mercantilist approach was sanctioned. That is, for the welfare of the internal economy, the importation of foreign goods was discouraged by way of high tariffs, even by embargoes on certain goods.

The fortress economy never succeeded in Italy. The depression was weathered with some success, but the real test came with war. Raw materials were lacking. Historically, the Italian social experience had no taste for Teutonic regimentation, and the corporate state, so comfortably beneath il Duce's thumb on paper, fell apart in reality. He was never able to dominate his conservative upper class, and just before his fall he lamented that it was the capitalists who had ruined his corporate state.

Germany Hitler's objectives were much the same as Mussolini's. He planned to suppress communism and gain control of industry for the purpose of building a conquering army. Economically, however, the setting was different. German industry was relatively self-sufficient and of an old and strong tradition. Also, unlike Mussolini's, much of Hitler's theorizing had to be made public before he gained power. During his years of political struggle, therefore, he was forced to condone attitudes far more leftist than his own. Other party leaders in the 1920s, particularly Hitler's prime rival Gregor Strasser, took the "socialism" in "national socialism" as a serious philosophy and not just a symbol for the sake of gaining adherents. While Hitler intended to keep business intact so long as it worked in the interest of war and expansion, Strasser wanted not only to nationalize big business but also to break up the big estates for the sake of the small peasant. Such a proposal was a severe embarrassment to Hitler in his quest for political support among the wealthy landowners and industrialists. Hitler's views would prevail, but, not one to forget old arguments, he saw to it that Strasser was shot along with other dissidents and troublemakers in the Roehm party and Storm Trooper purge of June, 1934.

From a practical point of view, Hitler was right. He would

need his industrialists during the critical campaigns of the early thirties. In 1932 he would address and impress the Industry Club where Fritz Thyssen, head of the Vereinigte Stahlwerke coal empire, was his avid supporter. Later Thyssen, too, would be cast aside, ending the war in a detention camp, but, with his initial support and the growing support of other industrialists, Hitler obtained the funds vital to his success. Established in power, his first moves seemed indeed to serve business interests, with the establishment of high mercantilist tariffs, the stimulation of public works projects, and a return to arms production.

Unlike Mussolini, Hitler undertook no artificial corporate structures, only the necessary controls to freeze the capitalistic system as it was, with preference for those large production units that almost uniformly linked their economic interests with Hitler's version of the fortress economy.

At first even the workers seemed to prosper. At least with rearmament and public works they were not idle, but by 1936 a total war economy had been established. Trade unions, collective bargaining, the right to strike—all were forbidden. The worker had become a virtual serf, with even his right to change jobs restricted. Not even his free time was his own, for through the "Strength through Joy" organization the state planned evening activities, clubs, and cheap (if regimented) vacations. The height of worker disillusionment came with the Volkswagen, "The People's Car." Every worker was to have one. It was to be mass-produced at 990 marks ($396) per car. Workers made regular payments, and once 750 marks was paid in by a worker, an order number was issued to him. The process was slow. No peoples' cars were forthcoming, and the story went around that one worker, despairing of ever getting his car through regular channels, stole one by one the parts and pieces that presumably would assemble into such a car. These he put together at home, only to find that he had constructed an armoured staff car. Facetious or not, before a single Volkswagen was delivered, total production went over to military goods and no refunds on down payments were made.

The small farmers fared a bit better. Part of the Fascist mystique was the praise of the agrarian life, and the memory that in World War I agriculture had fallen short of the country's need. The big Junker estates were not broken up, of course, as Hitler had led many smaller farmers to anticipate. Instead of being allocated portions of the big estates the small farmers were protected under a law that said their property could not be sold or foreclosed. In effect, they became pampered serfs subject to strict government regulation as to prices, when to fatten and market hogs, how to use their cultivated soil. Popular among them was the following attempt to differentiate between Socialists, Communists, and Germany's own National Socialists. If a farmer had six cows, the Socialists would demand three and leave the farmer three. The Communists would take the entire herd, while the German Fascists would let the farmer keep all the cows so long as they got all the milk.

The main concern of the war economy was naturally big business. Small business was a nuisance. Jewish business was rapidly Aryanized. This program applied especially to textiles and leather goods. Stockholder power was decreased and many small corporations were dissolved. Only the big industrial empires were favored, and they grew rapidly through the absorption of small concerns. Once the war was begun, foreign plants were taken over. One firm alone, I. G. Farben, which produced coal-tar dyes, chemicals, and explosives, came, in the course of the war, to dominate 380 German concerns, and it was additionally involved in 2,000 cartel agreements, many of them abroad.

German capitalists could make money, lots of it, but in terms of free enterprise, as defeat loomed, they were to become slaves, ordering about other slaves. Gradually, the Ministry of Economics and its many subdivisions, such as the Four-Year Plan Commission, the Price Control Commission, and the Labor

Service Administration, among many, put an end to volunteerism in industry. Jurisdictions were often overlapping or confused, with a fixed tendency for the state to dominate smaller firms more rigidly than larger, more powerful ones. Leadership was allowed initiative so long as it boosted production for the war effort. Stockholders tended to be rewarded with funds rather than control. Ideally, Hitler saw the economy as one big corporation with himself as permanent chairman of the board, but of course the crisis of wartime and the vastness and complexity of the interest groups involved kept this from materializing in rigid practice.

Whether because of the system or despite it, German industry continued to expand throughout the war. Fighter plane production was never higher than in 1944, but certain raw materials were running out. Vital oil fields were being reappropriated by the Soviet Army; oil shipments and refineries were being blasted by U.S. and British bombers to the point that there was no fuel to put the air armada into the sky. The fortress economy, along with the rest of "Fortress Europe," was going up in smoke.

Japan   If Japan had a fascist economy before and during World War II, it was not so much a function of an upsurge of fascist feeling and ideology as a result of traditional Japanese policy. An island nation, only recently thrown into the hurly-burly of international commerce, Japan had learned to take a suspicious mercantilist approach to foreign products. European-style imperialism as an outgrowth of capitalism was originally denounced, and the government controlled a rapid industrial growth, with direct incentives to heavy industry. Since the turn of the century Japan had geared itself to catching up with Western nations. The fortress economy that Mussolini and Hitler preached in the heart of Europe came very naturally to this tightly knit group of islands until population explosion made it unfeasible.

As early as 1897 a law had been passed in Japan making it compulsory for manufacturers in each branch of industry to form associations for the purpose of collectively overcoming deficiencies. This goal was clarified by the Major Industries Control law of 1931, which established control and cooperation in virtually every leading industry. Cartels set limits on total output and fixed individual production quotas, selling, pricing, and order allotments.

The industries of Japan had developed along family lines, some remaining small household affairs while others had grown into monstrous structures under paternalistic family direction. Forming pyramidal hierachies similar to Germany's I. G. Farben, four family cliques—Mitusi, Mitsubishi, Sumitomo, and Yasuda —dominated the economic structure. From the first they had cooperated in implementing Japan's developing policy of economic warfare and conquest, if for no other reason than that they owned, or at least controlled, big Japanese colonial development companies on the mainland of Asia, such as the South Manchurian Railroad Company. In this way the Japanese economic structure required very little adjustment to fascist ideology. It already had the industry that Italy lacked, nor was there the difficulty of accepting new political thinking and uncultivated leadership that was a hurdle the ignorant Austrian Hitler had to clear before winning the proud Prussian aristocrats to his ranks.

Fascism after World War II

Spain   Though militarily indebted to Italy and Germany, Spain took no part in World War II. Her own civil war had ended, as we have seen, in 1939 and she was in no condition to take part in another conflict. Spain lay in ruins and General Franco, his Church, his landowners, his army, and his Fascist Falange held the victory. Apart from the secret police, an efficient organization designed by the Nazi SS chief Himmler, and the execution squads, Spain was at a standstill. A quarter of a million prisoners languished in Jail. Five courts-martial were in permanent session in Madrid, and dawn after foggy dawn the convicted, their mouths muzzled with rubber straps so they could not shout republican defiance, were bundled by truck to the cemeteries. There they were marched on gangplanks over open pits into which they were dropped by machine-gun fire. One hundred thousand political prisoners died thus after the civil war. Many more died of starvation and disease in the bleak Spanish jails. Torture induced confessions, and when sentences seemed too lenient, there was no such protection as double jeopardy. A second trial was held. In method and cruelty, the Fascist concentration camps of Italy and Germany had little to teach the Spaniards. Yet Spain was not a Fascist land.

It was not a Fascist land even though its one surviving political party, the Falange, was Fascist, and might, with the restoration of peace, have been expected to rise to power in the political arena. The Falange, however, suffered from one great weakness compounded by a deadly mistake. The weakness could not be helped. Spanish industry had never been very advanced and the war had destroyed what there was of it, along with the industrial workers from whom any real leftist threat might arise. Victory for the Falange was self-defeating: it left no enemy to provide a purpose. The mistake was that of Mussolini, the blunder of which the Falange's executed founder, José Antonio de Rivera, had forewarned. In war, the party had sided with a more powerful ally, Franco and his army. It had fought against the mass of the Spanish people and in victory it was tied to the conservatives. Unlike Hitler, it had failed to conquer the streets and had to settle for a part in the "Francoist" coalition.

In 1939, robbed of much of its original direction and under Franco's thumb, the Falange became the basis for a new state. Officially, the goal was to establish an economic regime overriding the interests of class, group, or individual. There would be a one-party system within the state, its purpose to multiply wealth in the service of the state. If certain Falangists thought otherwise, there was always the army to reckon with.

The army occupied a very different position in Spain than it had in Germany or Italy. In the latter countries, social revolution had been achieved through Fascist politics. The army was traditionally conservative and had been willing to join the parade. In the end, it had become the weapon in the hands of successful revolution. In Spain, however, the officer corps had always regarded politics as its business. Under its direction the army, not the party, had won the revolution, and the army was loyal to its leaders. The civil war had culled out most of the older leadership, while those who survived owed their promotions to Franco. Franco was not unappreciative of his position. A tough, calculating, and pitiless soldier, he knew both how to dispose of threats to his power and how to use the army as a basis for canceling out the competitive aspirations of the Falange and the conservative Right of Church and aristocracy.

Franco's army was not simply a detached, garrisoned fighting force. It had small prospects of achieving glory through fascistic conquest. At most, the Falangists had African ambitions, and they demanded Gibraltar as they are still demanding Gibraltar. De Rivera had talked of links with the Hispanic people of Latin America, a kind of Latin Aryanism, but all these efforts were halfhearted at best. Meanwhile the decadent army had little to do except support its general. Officers were many and ill-paid, but they had advantages. Tied together by bonds of professional camaraderie, the army was a stepping-stone to other, better-paying civilian jobs that officers were permitted to hold while still in service. The army, in effect, was almost a union and employment service unto itself, and many a favored officer spent most of his days at a civil desk job while his orderly took his children out to the park to play.

While the army was settling in for the long and comfortable haul, the Falange was running out of options. Throughout World War II, with Hitler trying to win Franco over to his cause, the Spanish Fascists kept alive hopes of aid from Germany. Hitler's picture hung on the wall, and blue-shirted, red-bereted adolescents marched in anticipation of a Nazi victory and their own national revolution. But Spain's social war was over, and presently Hitler too was in retreat. Franco saw the handwriting on the wall. His tolerance for Falangist foolishness began to evaporate. In 1944 its salute was abolished. At the same time it was deprived of control over mass media, and a Ministry of Education took over. As the last Falangist hopes of overturning the regime faded, other minor parties began to fill the vacuum left by its disintegration.

Traditionally, Spain's one other structured center of power has been the Church. Of course, through fear of the godless priest-killing Reds who threatened not only life and limb but the Church's great economic, judicial, and social power as well, it sided with Franco during the civil war, and subsequently Franco has protected the Church as a historical relic. Spain remains a land of ritual if not of faith. Most teachers come from the Church, and the Chruch influences conservative textbooks, which regard liberalism as a sin against the faith. The Church controls the censorship of entertainment, the duration of a film kiss, but when opposed to Franco's civil authority, the Church is powerless, if for no better reason than money. The state controls the purse-strings, paying even the parish curates, and should a pastor act contrary to official policy, he would presently be fired by his bishop acting under government pressure.

Thought control, the rigid reshaping of education and the press, are Fascist characteristics. This control exists in Spain, but with a difference. The official policy has not been so much one of instilling new ideologies as it has been a negative process of "disintellectualization." The press, subject to a general press bureau, must espouse the official line or at least keep silent on the subject. The latter choice is most common. Education tends to be neglected and teachers underpaid. In the universities traditional dogma is preferred to research, and if a young man wants a practical education, his usual recourse is to the army, which offers practical schooling. There at least, illiterates are taught to read.

In dealing with the economy and labor, Franco has achieved a form of strict control not far removed from the Fascist ideal. Spain has always had a predominantly agrarian economy, comprised of feudal grandees and poor peasants. The civil war destroyed roads, railroad equipment, and factories, scarce raw materials were made unavailable even through importation during World War II, and the Spanish economy remained prostrate.

Franco's approach to this desperate situation was to combine the methods of Hitler and Mussolini. Hitler had set up a German labor front containing employers and employees, thereby achieving regimentation over the workers. In Italy there had been the Confederation of Fascist Corporations. While in Italy the link with the state had been direct, through the Ministry of Corporations, Franco followed the German pattern of putting the Falange in charge, as the Nazi party was in Germany. Under the Falange's direction, vertical syndicates, reminiscent of Italian fascism, were established, with such product groupings as olives, wine, cattle, fuel, and colonial goods. Within each syndicate, employer and employee were brought together. The party union was the only employment agency, and the right to work depended on membership. In this way the entire work force was subject to party control, and the party at local, provincial, and national levels remained subservient to the state and to Franco.

To work at all, let alone gain economic power and influence, a man had to join the party and become a part of the totalitarian system, a system so well controlled that if a spontaneous public demonstration in behalf of the government was desired to impress a visitor, each union or section was assigned a place to congregate in front of a given house before Franco and his foreign guests were scheduled to drive by. "Responsible" people took due note of those workers who turned out to cheer and those who did not, and by and large the foreign dignitary was treated to an enthusiastic welcome.

Over the years a veneer of "democratization" has been permitted. After 1951 workers were allowed to elect their leaders, the catch being that their choice was limited to a list approved by party officials. To make results doubly sure, the powers of the elected leaders remained consultative and in no way binding. In the early sixties the workers' unions began to test their strength. Strikes have occurred, and reprisals, and the general line of demarcation of toleration has been whether or not the issues were political. If purely a question of occupation, hours, pay, labor dissent, the government has been lenient. On the other hand, in keeping with Spain's traditional, authoritarian state, unaccustomed to industrialization, at the slightest suggestion of leftist or liberal politics the workers have been ruthlessly suppressed.

Unlike Germany or Italy, Spain has made no pretense of the "fortress economy." Without any hope of self-sufficiency, Spain has sought out foreign aid and in this respect has remained internationally a satellite of the United States, which has done much to retrieve Spanish economy from the doldrums. Despite the combined conservativism of Franco and the Church, technical progress has developed. Spain is rapidly becoming an industrialized and solvent nation of more or less contented, politically apathetic people. From what was once very close to Nazi-style totalitarianism, Spain has moved gradually toward paternal authoritarianism under Franco. Under his anticipated successor, the modifying trend has every reason to continue.

Portugal Spain's western neighbor, Portugal, has been identified with fascism. Portuguese fascism, however, was not derived from a bloody civil war, as in Spain, nor was it torn down by world conflict, as in the Fascist states of Western Europe. Politically Portugal has kept outside the mainstream of political and economic events and has essentially remained a preindustrial nation. In such conditions there has grown up no basis for leftist worker challenge to traditional authoritarianism, and hence no pressure for a mass fascistic reaction. But as is typical of all fascism, it has had one outstanding leader, Antonio de Oliveira Salazar, a most untypical dictator. Neither ambitious general nor aspiring politician and mob leader, he was only an obscure economics professor from Coimbra University.

In the mid 1920s Portugal was an impoverished republic beset by unrest and abortive military revolts. With an appeal to the people in behalf of national dignity and honor, General Gomes da Costa launched one of these revolts on May 28, 1926.

This time the ruling Democratic party was cast out with scarcely a casualty. A governing triumvirate was set up, and Dr. Salazar was brought in to sort out the financial mess. His public appearance was brief. The military was quickly dissatisfied, the government was overturned, and the nonpolitical Salazar was back on campus. Not until 1928 did he return permanently to public life. By this time General Antonio Oscar Carmona was president, and he recalled Salazar as a last hope for propping up Portugal's financial house, as lack of funds, not warring ideologies, was the country's cause of continuing crisis.

Almost with reluctance this thin, pale, black-clad teacher left his classroom. He lacked entirely the hysterical thunder of Hitler, the strutting showmanship of Mussolini, but he would outlast them both. Used to austerity, he continued to lead a modest life. Pomp and ceremony meant nothing to him, and when he broke his leg, he insisted on paying the medical bills personally. Called on to make a public speech, he did so quietly, without histrionics, addressing specific, dry problems. He never promised Portugal the world, but he was a hermit with very definite political and economic ideas and a competent housekeeper.

His first undertaking, while still only a finance minister, was to draw up a project paper for resuscitating the Portuguese economy. This program he called "Conditions of Financial Reform," but it was much more: an entire theory of government in which he called for a dictatorship, emphasizing the nation above the individual or the state. From the beginning he rejected the racist ideas of Germany, the class conflict emphasized by Soviet Russia, and the party foundation represented by Italy. Salazar advocated a União Nacional (National Union), to be a pressure group binding the community in a corporate movement.

On July 5, 1932, Salazar was elevated to prime minister, and within a year his corporate constitution was on the books. Ideally, it envisioned a unitary rather than a conflicting pluralistic society. There was to be something of Mussolini's corporativism, seasoned with the ideas of the medieval guild. There would be no class struggles, no strikes or lockouts. Syndicates of workers would be grouped in federations, depending on their particular trade or industry. Above these would be unions, represented by different, but connected and affiliated branches of a particular trade or industry, and at the top of this pyramid would be workers and employers in a national corporative chamber of government. While in Mussolini's corporate state system the flow of orders was envisioned from the top down, Salazar, at least in theory, saw representative government welling up from below, with the state taking a secondary role as servant, not as an end in itself.

Along with the corporative chamber to give representation in a vertical fashion, there was to be an assembly elected nationally, thereby giving what Salazar imagined to be horizontal representation. It all sounded very good on paper, but in practice few complete corporations developed and few members were ever appointed to the chamber. With his paper system lagging behind his hopes, Salazar was becoming a dictator. In practice the government was not answerable to the parliament for its executive acts, and the only man who might turn Salazar as prime minister out of office was the president, chosen by election every seven years.

Lest such a challenge develop, it was Salazar's practice to select the candidate for president from among his supporters. But in 1958 came opposition led by General Humberto Delgado. He criticized the high profit rate of the industrialists, the meager salaries of the wage earners, Salazar's fear of accepting foreign aid, and his very slow, un-Keynesian, pay-as-you-go formula. Despite police hindrance and stern censorship, Delgado fought a courageous fight for the presidency and managed to gain a quarter of the votes cast. The cost was heavy. Presently dismissed from the army, Delgado turned unsuccessfully to the time-honored military coup. In 1961 with piratical flair he seized the cruise ship *Santa Maria*. Even this grand gesture came to nothing, and soon afterward he ended his career in a shallow grave just across the Spanish border.

No challenger rose to replace him. Salazar ruled on until 1968, when a stroke (to be followed by natural death) pulled him from the seat of power. Without dramatics, Professor Marcello des Neves Alves Caetano took over as prime minister.

The question remains, was Salazar a Fascist dictator? Did he establish a Fascist state, or only a condition of medieval paternalism? The answer depends on the definition of fascism. Certainly many ingredients were and still are present. First there was the fear of communism, an obsession with Salazar. There was his countering ideology, the corporate society, more a matter of theory than fact. There were elements of Fascist technique such as censorship, but without the pervasive efforts at mind control demonstrated by the Nazis. As early as 1936, there was the Mocidade Portuguesa, a youth group reminiscent of the Nazi Youth, although far less widspread. Finally, there was PIDE, Policia Internacional e de Defesa do Estado. This was Salazar's version of the Gestapo, and it gave a brutal turn to his administration. Salazar tried to justify PIDE's existence because of the Communist threat, which was a convienient name for any threat to his rule. Finally, one might point to Portugal's African colony Angola, the last major colony in Africa, as an example of Fascist imperialism, but only in its tenacity does this imperialism differ from the former policies of more democratic powers. In essence, then, the distinction between the Portuguese system and other Fascist governments is one of degree, with one material exception. True fascism sees war and conquest as the final mission of the corporate state. Salazar, on the other hand, despised this goal and conversely imagined his system as diminishing ethnic and class conflict.

Argentina   After World War II Argentina became a refuge for many fleeing Nazis. Its aspirations had been linked with those of Germany and its armies were imagined to be preparing for the conquest of South America. Much of this was myth, magnified and made to seem real by wartime fears and propaganda, but Argentina did experience a political episode with more Fascist elements than are common in the several military dictatorships of Latin America.

To begin with, Argentina was always strongly nationalistic from the time when its great liberator, José de San Martín, drove out the Spanish governor in 1816. A variety of governments would follow independence. Some brought reform, others simply army rule. In 1829 arrived Juan Manuel de Rosas, and to him is attributable a tradition of xenophobic nationalism, for Rosas did his best to keep out foreign capital, enterprise, and immigration, even foreign cultural influences. Though he was in his turn overthrown, he established a pattern.

Nearly a century later, in the 1920s, Argentina experienced a revival of Rosasism, along with a growing antidemocratic mood prompted by Mussolini and the Spain of Primo de Rivera. Among the military there was a rising sense of mission to restore Argentina and lift her from the humiliation of corrupt and ineffectual civilian governors. Depression came in 1929 and the crisis neared. On September 4 of the following year General José F. Uriburu took over in a nearly bloodless coup. Uriburu was a Fascist, and he was determined to establish a corporate state administered by a military elite. Unfortunately for Uriburu, his following was small. Even part of the army opposed him, and within a year he was displaced by military conservatives— not Fascists really, but generals disposed to neutrality, friendship with Germany, and a challenge to United States leadership in Latin America. This affront to the United States made the generals and their successors seem Fascist to the North American press and public.

Typically, the generals achieved order, but they had no talent for governing. The politicians who replaced them did no better, and in 1943 yet another military coup, one that received little support and less opposition from the public, put the Grupo de Oficiales Unidos (the United Officers Group) in power. A minor member of this military clique was Colonel, later General, Juan Perón. His share of the spoils was the presidency of the Department of Labor. In this post his first fame came when he drummed up massive aid for the victims of a severe earthquake. At the same time he set about building up a nationwide trade union movement out of formerly weak independent unions.

Perón's success with the mob was by no means gratifying to his colleagues. In 1945 they deprived him of his post, but they had delayed too long. Perón chose to defy the GOU (United Officers Group) and called on his workers, his "shirtless ones," for support. Reminiscent of Hitler's Storm Troopers, they marched by torchlight, and with their flaming support Perón announced his candidacy for president.

His meteoric rise was an interesting inversion of Mussolini's Blackshirt days. While Mussolini beat down the workers, Perón was uplifted by them. While Mussolini dramatized his Fascist power by assuming control in the face of a leftist general strike, Perón made his point by commanding such a strike. Truckloads of "shirtless" youths smashed up stores, stoned opponents' campaign trains, and broke up their rallies. Still, it took the blundering interference of the United States to push him into the presidency. Hoping to hurt his election chances, the United States rushed a "Blue Book" into print that contained alleged proof of Perón's Axis affiliations. Rallying with cries of "Yankee intervention," the book was all that Perón needed to win.

His first term as president ran from 1946 to 1952. At this time his power was based securely on the labor force and less securely upon the army. His professed objective for Argentina was genuine democracy. Domestically, he spoke of economic independence and threatened to expropriate foreign interests and big estates. These promises were generally not carried through. The estates continued to dominate the rural scene and the expropriation of foreign interests, notably the British-run railroad system, came only after generous compensation. In principle, Perón believed the state should intervene in the economy to safeguard the general interest, but in practice results were less along lines of national socialism than pure socialism. The result was that public and private capital became mixed.

What was most truly fascistic about the Perón regime was the violent mass support for his charismatic leadership, and that of his wife Eva, even though the base for this support was contrary to true fascism, which draws its shock troops from the conservative lower-middle class. Perón depended upon the workers, the usual hard core of the Left, in what has been called proletarian fascism. If reminiscent of anything, it was the national socialism of Gregor Strasser, which Hitler had so emphatically repudiated. More in keeping with the fascism of Hitler and Mussolini were the repressive measures applied by Perón to consolidate his power. While the workers received large Christmas bonuses to keep them loyal, other social institutions were quickly brought under control. *La Prensa,* the revered and honored newspaper of Argentina, was seized, along with the radio. Opposition congressmen were dismissed for disorderly conduct. The universities were taken over and uncooperative faculty members dropped, as were opposition members of the Supreme Court. Lest these oppressions provoke hostilities, Perón looked for a common cause. As well as the forging of a new and respected Argentina, he needed a common enemy. Here he had trouble. There was no Jewish question in Argentina, no ethnic problem at all, and, with the workers solidly behind him, he could hardly raise the Communist menace. The best he could think of was North American imperialism and international financial exploitation, remote at best from the life of the average citizen.

This lack of a genuine foe would hurt him. The fact that his strength lay with the workers rather than the traditional power centers, business and the army, would also hurt. Then, too, there was his Hitleresque ineptitude in respect to finance. By 1952 and the beginning of his second term, Argentina was gripped by a severe depression. Perón had no recourse but to seek a rapprochement with the business community. At the same time he unwisely affronted national pride by signing an agreement with the Standard Oil Co. of California to exploit Argentinian petroleum.

His last mistake, in 1954, was to attack the strong Roman Catholic Church. His excommunication the following year was a signal to the military to rise in resistance. On September 15, 1955, the navy declared itself against Perón. Rather than promote a Spanish-style civil war, he fled on a Paraguayan gunboat. Though he was a military man, Perón's brand of proletarian fascism had failed to bind this vital base of power—which alone sets his movement outside the conventional definition of fascism.

Where elements of the Germany army had tried and failed to get rid of Hitler, the Argentine armed forces had succeeded with very little bloodshed in ousting Perón. They could not so easily dispel his spirit or the loyalty of his workers, nor have they been able to find an adequate substitute. Without the threat of military intervention, Perón would soon have returned. This the generals had not been willing to allow, so, in place of Perón's version of national socialism, they were left with a drifting form of military dictatorship which fostered economic decay and the development of a savage guerrilla movement. In the 1973 election a Perónist puppet, Hector J. Cámpora, was elected president. He retained the office for a brief fifty days, then resigned to permit Perón to be elected president in a special election. His supporters hoped he would lift Argentina to what they remember as its former glory. At age seventy-seven, in failing health and with the army still a strong political factor, it would seem he lacked the talent or administrative instinct to do what would be necessary.

South Africa   The Republic of South Africa, and, to a lesser extent, Rhodesia, are instances of repressive societies that are called Fascist simply because they are repressive and because the other popular Western smear word, Communist, doesn't fit even superficially. Of course a number of Fascist characteristics are present. They can be found to a greater or lesser extent in any country, and it is the purpose of the following to point them out, together with those features of the governmental and social structure that are contrary to traditional fascism.

That portion of southern Africa now occupied by the Republic of South Africa was originally inhabited solely by black tribes. A seventeenth-century trickle of European settlers had grown to an English and Dutch flood by the nineteenth. The Dutch, calling themselves "Afrikaners," were in the majority, but the British, referred to derisively as "outlanders," represented the more powerful empire. When it came to a clash in 1899, the British Empire prevailed and the British colony was expanded. Subsequently turned into an independent republic, South Africa's population remained 80 percent black. Among the white 20 percent the Afrikaners were in the majority. The whites owned nearly 90 percent of the land, but they needed black labor. All was quiet until the Second World War and the rapid rise of war industry. The process led to detribalization, urbanization, modernization, and some education for the blacks. The pastoral days were over, and there was no turning back.

The white British minority favored integration. The Afrikaners, however, feared liberalization, and in 1947 their Nationalist party came to power. Their policy was simple: to maintain control by 1,800,000 Afrikaners over 1,200,000 English-speaking South Africans and 13,000,000 nonwhites. Officially, this policy is called apartheid. In theory, it is not very different from the "separate but equal" segregation that was sanctioned by the Supreme Court of the United States until 1954, and which is still clung to desperately, particularly by the states of the deep South.

Apartheid did not materialize overnight. It had a hallowed if informal tradition going back to Cape Town in 1660, when a wild almond hedge was planted on a hill over the town and no Hottentot was permitted to pass it. The term itself is more recent, having been coined in 1944 by Prime Minister Daniel Malan. (It means "apartness" or "separation.") Apartheid had as its objective absolute separation of ethnic groups: separate accommodations, separate hospitals, separate beaches, separate schools. Everything was separate even institutions for treatment of the blind who couldn't care less about skin coloration. To say the least, apartheid proved wasteful, with accident victims bleeding to death in the street for want of the right-colored ambulance.

As a supplement to apartheid, Prime Minister Hendrik F. Verwoerd instituted his policy of "Separate Development." In this he insisted upon dealing with the old tribal leaders while boycotting the more modern African nationalist leadership which, of course, represents black Africa of today and tomorrow.

To implement these twin approaches to suppression of the blacks, laws were needed, and for such laws a single-minded electorate and legislature. To this end the Nationalist party, made up of white Afrikaners, pushed through the legislature a law removing Cape Coloured (Asiatics and people of mixed white and black ancestry) voters from the common roll of voters. To so amend the constitution, however, a two-thirds majority was needed, and so the Supreme Court struck down the law. Undaunted, the Nationalists established a new "High Court of Parliament." Again the Supreme Court held this maneuver invalid. Finally the white majority simply enlarged the Senate, made sure that 77 of the 89 House seats were filled by Nationalists, and thus presented the Supreme Court with more than a two-thirds majority. The Coloreds vanished from the voting rolls through tactics grimly reminiscent of Hitler's rise to power.

As with Hitler, laws were not enough. South Africa needed a power structure, and this developed none too quickly. Black resistance, implemented by white sympathizers, was growing. The police force expanded as well and was empowered to move anywhere on a nationwide basis. Protest riots occurred during the 1950s and were officially attributed to Communist agitators taking advantage of the "savages." Communism has never been a genuine concern in South Africa, but its value as a slogan opponent for world opinion was not overlooked.

By 1960 unrest had approached crisis when in Sharpeville 69 blacks were shot. Subsequently revolutionary activity was ruthlessly crushed, and by 1964 all major revolutionary organizations had been broken up and their leaders imprisoned. Liberally interpreted sabotage laws were enacted, making it almost impossible for blacks to congregate in groups. No black without a pass could stay in an urban area for over seventy-two hours, and if his pass was lost or stolen he could go to jail or be shipped out of the area. Furthermore, a public safety act empowered the government to declare a state of emergency at its own discretion. Having done so, arrests could be made without warrant and detention would follow "in the interest of public order for the duration of the state of emergency." Again, one is reminded of the "night and fog" decrees that allowed Hitler's Gestapo to drag off suspects without warning, and in most cases without their ever being heard of again.

With active internal resistance crushed, white South Africa was still up against world opinion and protests from the United Nations. Though silenced, the sullen black majority could not be forgotten, nor could the black neighboring states. To counter such fears, the police force was supplemented by the most formidable modern army in sub-Saharan Africa.

In one further respect, its "Broederbond" ("bond of brothers"), South Africa resembles Nazi Germany. The Broederbond was formed in 1918. It comprised the leading members of the

Afrikaner society and was initially dedicated to cultural objectives. Within a decade its purpose was "dominance" and its
membership, about four thousand, aided one another in civil
service promotion. The initiation ceremony involved stabbing a
knife into a dummy representing a corpse and declaring, "He
who betrays the Bond will be destroyed by the Bond." In the
early 1930s, this clique developed enthusiasm for the Nazi party
and its tactics and even promoted a youth movement along Hitler Youth lines called the "Voortrekkers." Other parallel devel-
opments were a student movement, "Afrikaner Studentebond,"
and a militant youth corps, the "Ruiterjag." Today the Broederbond would disavow any such Fascist tendencies, but the fact
remains it is a semisecret society made up of cabinet ministers,
party officials, and church leaders, of immense influence within
South Africa. Their purposes are twofold: their own promotion,
and the suppression of the black masses. In effect they are
nothing more than a high-brow version of the Ku Klux Klan.

South Africa and her neighbor Rhodesia are often lumped
together as examples of present-day fascism. Until 1965 Rhodesia was a self-governing colony within the British Common-
wealth. In that year it made a unilateral and unconstitutional
declaration of independence. This decision was prompted by
pressure from Britain and the United Nations to modify its constitution to bring equality to the black majority of the population. Fearing such equality might in the end mean white extinction, the Rhodesian Front, led by Ian Smith, proclaimed
independence and at the same time introduced a new constitution designed to shore up white dominion. Thus far, despite oil
embargos and freezing of funds, Rhodesia has successfully, if
less dramatically, followed in South Africa's footsteps.

For all of this, neither Rhodesia nor the Republic of South
Africa are Fascist states. Lacking are some of the essential ingredients of true fascism. First, there is no genuine fear of communism. Though this fear is exploited as a reason, it is fear of
the black millions that is the true motive. Second, there has

been no restructuring of the economic community toward the corporate state, fascism's customary answer to the Communist alternative. Next, these two countries are not militant in the sense of seeking territorial expansion. At best, they can hope to hold what they have. Finally, there is no massive support for either government. More aptly than "fascism," the system of government invented by South Africa might be called "police pigmentocracy," with status and civil rights a function of skin tone.

Thus far, at the price of fear and in some cases of guilt, the expensive system has worked. The whites remain solidly on top of the black millions. How long this stability can be maintained is the question asked by many close observers who regard those black millions as a volcano.

Fascism in the United States

The United States is not a Fascist country. It never was and it isn't likely to become one, but social groups within the country have shown a preference for right-wing extremism whenever they have felt themselves deprived of wealth, status, or influence. And today the country still has Fascists and groups with motivations and characteristics unhealthily fascistic. Even such red-blooded Americans as Theodore Roosevelt endorsed an economic philosophy that might, had it been implemented, have given a foretaste of national socialism. This "new nationalism," deriving from Herbert Croly's book *The Promise of American Life,* came as a reaction to the threat of progressivism and was the basis of Roosevelt's 1912 campaign for President. In the national interest, it called for an end of free competition in big business, favoring instead the creation of business monopolies under strict federal control. Putting aside the passions associated with later professed fascism, here was a forerunner of fascist corporate economics, which of course became academic when Roosevelt lost to a reform-minded Woodrow Wilson.

Twenty years later Theodore's cousin, Franklin D. Roosevelt, became President. The Great Depression had reduced the economy to rock bottom, and never had faith in democracy sunk so low. People were willing to clutch at straws, and among those straws was fascism. Even some of Franklin Roosevelt's measures to revive the economy, such as the National Recovery Administration, designed to link government and business in the country's interest, have been subsequently damned as fascistic. Although this was not the case, they were declared at the time unconstitutional by the Supreme Court and today professional Roosevelt-haters are more apt to revile the man as a Communist.

Fascistic Trends in the Thirties   The appeal of fascistic solutions to America's economic woes was shown in the meteoric popularity of a Canadian-born priest, Father Charles Coughlin, who gravitated to Detroit in 1921 and there used the *Catholic Hour* to air his views over the radio. Until 1930 he stuck to religion. Then he organized the Radio League of the Little Flower and launched a rhetorical tirade on politics, economics, and society. He became nationally popular, receiving eighty thousand letters a week. Like Hitler, his messages were emotional and persuasive. Like Hitler attacking the Versailles Treaty, Coughlin went after bankers and the lack of what he called social justice. Like Hitler, he was not above propagandistic tricks such as planting a bomb in his own basement to suggest an attack on his life, or urging over the radio as a Christian concern the restoration of silver to its proper value while he hoarded half a million ounces of silver.

Coughlin's movement was based on poverty and the depression. His following was made up of the victims of small business and farm failures, but even more so of unemployed manual workers. From a sociological viewpoint, this made it more of a "proletarian fascism" along the later Perónist lines than the lower-middle-class fascism exploited by Hitler and

Mussolini. By the mid 1930s Coughlin's movement boasted a membership in excess of the combined American Socialist and Communist parties. Calling itself the National League for Social Justice, the movement formed a strong Washington, D.C., pressure group. In general, its objectives were similar to the corporate state goals of Mussolini. In fact, in May, 1938, Coughlin's periodical, *Social Justice,* nominated Mussolini the man of the week. It defended his attacks on Abyssinia and advocated policies that were anti–trade union, anticommunist, and in favor of the corporate state. To all this Coughlin added a touch of anti-Semitism with the international Jewish banker as villain.

Coughlin's pressure group never succeeded in becoming a political party as he had hoped and these fascistic objectives were not realized, but his urgings that the United States keep away from involvement in the World Court and from the reorganization of the League of Nations were strong isolationistic influences at a time when greater world involvement might have forestalled the coming war. Even after hostilities had broken out in Europe, the Fascist priest praised Hitler and blamed the Jews for the war. In 1942, after the United States had become involved, he was told by church authorities to desist from political comment or be defrocked. Coughlin was silenced for good.

Another all-American with a manner like il Duce was Huey "the Kingfish" Long, governor of Louisiana. Long was loved by the poor people of his state, for he himself was a red-necked farmer who had made good, a nobody who bossed everybody. Superficially at least, Long was a southern populist whose loyalties allegedly were to the left of the Democratic New Deal of the early 1930s. But many regard him as an embryonic Fascist whose career, had it gone on long enough, would have taken him far to the Right. Whatever his loyalties, Long's methods were worthy of fascism, and within the confines of his poor and backward state he established the closest thing to a dictatorship the United States has ever known.

Like Hitler, his appeal was direct to the so-called will of

the people and his methods were repression and intimidation. He controlled the state's legislature and supreme court. A typical legislative bill-passing session saw Huey signing unread bills at the rate of one every two minutes while his legislators stood wordlessly by, coughing and clearing their throats. In this way Long managed to streamline the state government, shift the burden of tax from the poor, build highways, and improve the schools. Like Hitler, he believed in a forceful display. His police were always on parade, particularly during election time, when they were ready to seize voting lists, arrest "dangerous" opponents, and see that the outcome suited Long.

Long recorded the names of his enemies in a little "Son-of-a-Bitch Book" and a notation usually meant an imminent increase in the assessment of the offender's property. In the case of opposition newspapers, Huey established a 2 percent tax on their gross receipts for advertising, saying, "This tax should be called a tax on lying, two cents per lie."

This colorful demagogue had ambitions far beyond the bayous of Louisiana. He became a United States senator, a hopeful step toward the presidency, which he further advanced with a national Share-the-Wealth Program. This scheme envisioned reducing big fortunes, dividing up property, and nationalizing industry in the interest of pensions for the old and minimum work for all. As his expressed intention, this was something to please the mob. Like Mussolini, he also indulged in dramatic public works to lend credence to his leftist-seeming demagoguery while in practice he maintained a system of conservative privileges. Despite all his leftist talk, Long never put through a minimum-wage or child labor law, unemployment insurance or old age pensions. Children were left to work in the shrimp-packing plants and strawberry fields while his overt taxation of large corporations was offset in most cases by reduced assessments on their properties. He was not immune to bribes from business and was noted for his cooperation with big industrialists such as the Mellon and DuPont families. Like Hitler and Mussolini, he knew where the power was and that he must cooperate with it. He also had the wisdom to remark that if fascism ever came to the United States, it would come under the slogan of one hundred percent Americanism.

By 1935 Long's presidential aspirations had ripened. That summer his ghost writers were working on his book, *My First Years in the White House,* where he planned to replace both Democratic and Republican parties with his own organization. Huey did not lack for confidence. To discredit the administration, on August 9 he made a speech in the United States Senate in which he read into the record a transcript allegedly taken from a hidden dictaphone that asserted there was an administration plot to have him murdered before the 1936 elections. After this, Long returned to Louisiana for fence-mending, which was to include the ousting of one of his most resolute enemies, Judge Ben Pavy. This objective was to be achieved in part by indicating that the judge had Negro blood, an accusation as damning in Louisiana as a similar suspicion of Jewish blood would have been in Nazi Germany. This scheme evidently drove the judge's son-in-law, Dr. Carl Austin Weiss, to madness when he learned of it, for on September 8 he waylaid Long in the Baton Rouge State House. Here he got off one fatal shot before being cut to pieces by the bullets of Long's bodyguards.

How far the Kingfish would have climbed but for the doctor's good aim, how far he would have moved from a populist façade to a fascistic reality, must remain an unanswered question. A suggestion comes from the career of Long's second-in-command and the organizer of his Share-the-Wealth Program, Gerald Smith. Up until Long's death Smith spoke of this movement sweeping the nation and duplicating the "feat of Adolf Hitler in Germany."

Prior to joining Long's team, Gerald Smith had belonged to another, avowedly Fascist group, the Silver Shirts, a name not accidently derived from Hitler's Blackshirts, or SS. The Silver Shirts, a West Coast phenomenon of the depression and never very powerful, had been founded by William Dudley Pelley. Pelley was not one to mince words. He believed in Fascist dictatorship achieved by violence, in the suppression of trade unions, and the support of industry. His eventual goal economically was to turn the nation into one huge corporation, with each citizen getting a share. Negroes, Indians, "aliens" (meaning primarily Jews) were to become wards of the government. Internal dissensions and personal animosities among the Silver Shirt hierarchy would keep the organization from growing to dangerous proportions. Gerald Smith was one of the first to defect when he headed south to team up with Long. After Long, he would move on to assist Father Coughlin.

The Longs, the Pelleys, the Coughlins all flirted with aspects of fascism, American style, and they were all hindered by the character of the people they tried to manipulate. Anything smacking of European borrowings, as Long had noted, was un-American and generally unacceptable. Then, too, the American people have always been solidly against the recognition of class, the sociological foundation upon which any true Communist-Fascist struggle is based. From the very beginning, the United States has emphasized individual achievement over class or group identification. All of this makes it very difficult for true fascism to gain a foothold unless it twists itself around and champions some apparently all-American virtue such as opposition to big business or big government.

The Ku Klux Klan   Predating European fascism but sharing its taste for lavish symbols, violence, prejudice, and regional, if not national, chauvinism, is the Ku Klux Klan. This is a strictly American organization that thrived between the two world wars under the guise of all-Americanism. The Klan was born in December of 1865 in the small market center of Pulaski, Tennessee. If one is to believe the folk stories, it began playfully enough when some young Confederate war veterans decided to form a club and haunt an old deserted farmhouse. This they did, and in the process they roused rumors of ghosts and almost inadvertently frightened the local Negroes. Older and less playful men saw value in this reaction as a means of controlling the postwar and lawless South while curtailing the liberal policies proposed by the North. General Nathan Bedford Forrest became the Grand Wizard of the Klan, and the organization grew into a vigilante group, professing to protect the weak and the innocent and to uphold the Constitution.

By 1869 the Klan had drifted into more violent hands, and blacks and northern "carpetbaggers" were being savagely treated. The costumes were different—white robes, peaked hoods—but otherwise the atmosphere was very much like that which existed in Germany and Italy after World War I. Postwar impoverishment coupled with the influx of liberals from the North encouraged many Southerners, both lower- and upper-class, to support this terrorist guerrilla effort in behalf of the status quo. As its more violent elements grew, its more moderate leadership became disillusioned. General Forrest ordered "the Invisible Empire" to disband, but the reign of terror persisted into the 1870s, when the end of the Reconstruction period removed most of those pressures that the Klan resisted.

Over forty years would pass. Then the film *The Birth of a Nation,* glorifying the old Klan, together with Thomas Dixon's book *The Clansman: An Historic Romance of the Ku Klux Klan,* would stir old memories and bring into focus new frustrations among the conservative lower-middle class. In 1915 the Klan was chartered by the state of Georgia, a poor state that felt itself exploited by northern industry. The end of World War I, which brought to a close America's first brief flirtation with internationalism, introduced a reaction against all things un-American. The country was seen to be in a process of moral decay. Immigrants and Negroes returning from the war were expected to vie for the few available jobs. Jews, anarchists, Catholics, labor union strikers, Reds, alcoholics, all were combining to drag the country to damnation. With a sense of moral rectitude and a call for law and order, the village bigot donned his hooded costume. Well represented were the Protestant clergy and the police amid ranks that swelled, by 1924, to dominate the political scene in the following states: Oregon, Oklahoma, Texas, Arkansas, Indiana, Ohio, and California. Nationwide, the Klan boasted a membership of 2 million.

The Klan dreamed of running the country and of extending membership abroad. With its attraction of anti-Semitism, it even set up a branch in Berlin. In 1926 a Canadian chapter succeeded in bombing a Catholic church in Ontario, but in general its appeal was limited to the United States and particularly to the South. By the 1930s its hatred of everything foreign, everything not Anglo-Saxon, everything not Aryan in the Nazi sense of the word, produced a natural affinity for the burgeoning Fascist parties of Europe. The Klan developed a palm-downward fascistic salute, opposed the United States involvement in the Permanent Court of International Justice, and by 1940 was sufficiently attracted to nazism that the two held a joint rally at Camp Nordland, New Jersey.

By this time, however, the Klan was already on the decline. Its Nazi affinity didn't help it at home, nor did its corrupt, greedy, and generally uncharismatic leadership. More important, however, was a kind of defeat through victory. Many of its objectives (such as prohibition, keeping the Negro war veteran from upsetting the status quo, and legislation against immigration) had been achieved, thereby seeming to relieve the threat to the conservative status quo. With the Second World War the Klan appeared doomed to utter extinction, an impression that would persist until 1954 and the Supreme Court decision on school integration.

Fascism in the United States was not limited to related organizations and demagogues. In the 1930s a German-American Bund, with its "Ordnungs Dienst" (Storm Troopers) was growing, but, as Huey Long had observed, its very foreignness held it back. This the American Nazis tried to overcome by organizing the American Nationalist party, which played down the swastika and pushed Americanism. The party had rather unrealistic hopes of taking over the government. Its members paraded as super-patriots and propagandized against Communists, which in their lexicon included Jews, liberals, New Dealers, and labor organizations. At its peak the party magazine, *Social Justice,* passed a weekly circulation of 1 million. The war, of course, put an end to professed nazism in the United States, and only a contemptibly small band of fanatics have continued to sport swastikas since the war.

Wars turn unlikely allies into a band of brothers. In the peace that follows, old and forgotten differences are again recognized and, through disillusionment, often exaggerated. This was the case with World War II, and the "Cold War" that followed created a nightmare of Communist subversion worthy of Hitler's Germany. Had economic depression rather than continued prosperity accompanied this mood, there is no telling what might have happened to American democracy. As it was, democracy was shaken. Even that last bastion of individual rights, the Supreme Court, upheld the constitutionality in peacetime of the 1940 Smith Act, whereby the simple advocacy of the duty, necessity, or propriety of revolution was held to be a criminal offense. Good men were blacklisted, books were burned.

The McCarthy Era   This state of suspicion and accusation of all opposition as Communist-inspired came to be called "McCarthyism." McCarthyism was not a movement or a party. Joseph McCarthy, United States senator from Wisconsin, was no leader. He offered no economic program or philosophy, but he focused a conservative tendency of the times. Another war, the one in Korea, had again unsettled the social structure. Curiously, it was a time of prosperity, a time of new millionaires feeling insecure about their sudden wealth. A depression was expected but did not come, but the principal fear came from afar, from the Soviet Union. Fascism had all too recently been the world enemy, but now it was communism that loomed larger in the world than it ever had before.

It was McCarthy, warning of an alleged Communist conspiracy to dominate the world and the United States from within as well as from without, who brought these conservative agonies bubbling to the surface. Except for the undemocratic and accusatory methods used to exploit the fear of this threat from the Left, McCarthyism was not fascist, but the situation that developed about him illustrates how a government of sane men, steeped in democratic tradition and constitutionality, can be pushed toward the frenzied state of mind that makes fascism possible.

Joseph McCarthy arrived in Washington as junior senator from Wisconsin in 1946. At that time he liked to characterize himself as a marine tail gunner who had risen through the ranks. In fact he had entered the service with a commission and fired his only shots, 4,700 rounds, from the machine guns of a grounded dive bomber sitting at the end of a runway. His target has never been ascertained, but it was not communistic. In fact, there was little about the man in 1946 to suggest that within four years he would rise through means of naked allegations to become the symbol of the one force in the United States that was resisting overthrow by the Reds.

There were some early hints of his distaste for protocol and the rules of the Senate. Basically McCarthy was hungry for recognition and power. He had no time to rise by hard work through the system, and by 1950 there seemed a good chance he would be unseated in the 1952 election unless he built a record on some issue. McCarthy's first idea was to promote a pension plan for the elderly, but this was old hat. From Edmund Walsh, dean of the Georgetown School of Foreign Service, came the suggestion he attack Communists in government. The time was ripe. The cold war was at its peak, and the fear of radicalism had deep roots going back to labor riots, Sacco and Vanzetti, and the horror of Bolsheviks that developed after the First World War.

With a taste for breathless extremities, McCarthy began his attack early in 1950 with an address to a West Virginia Republican ladies group. During the talk he held up a bundle of papers, shouting, "I have here in my hand a list of 205 names known to the Secretary of State as being Communists still shaping policy in the State Department." What he had, in fact, was a list of 285 names out of 3,000 screened employees who had for various reasons not been recommended for permanent employment by the department. Of these, 79 were no longer employed, leaving 205, in McCarthy's terms, "Communists." Publicity and reaction were nationwide. Those who disputed his claims became "egg-sucking phony liberals" or "dupes of the Kremlin."

McCarthy, although a demogogue like Hitler, lacked Hitler's talent for grand political strategy. He was a one-issue person, limited to causing sensational upheaval and confusion, and his capability was much enhanced by the mass media's chronic desire to sell sensationalism. He came at a critical time, the advent of the Korean War. In the Red scare that ensued, the McCarran Internal Security Act was proposed by Republicans, aimed at registering members of the Communist party and drastically undercutting traditional liberties guaranteed by the First and Fifth Amendments to the Constitution. Not to be outdone, Democratic liberals proposed an alternative bill, providing for the emergency detention and internment of suspected subversives. Remembered as the "concentration camp bill," it was fortunately bypassed. The McCarran bill, however, was approved by the Senate 70 to 7.

McCarthy's attacks extended far beyond the "red-tinted" State Department. By 1953, as head of the Committee on Government Operations, he had become the grand inquisitor, going after the Voice of America, which he asserted was full of "Communists, left-wingers, New Dealers, radicals and pinkos." Typically, his allegations were startling, and they were based upon documentation that, when exposed, turned out to be old data, misinterpreted or actually rewritten. These dubious tactics, when questioned, were simply buried by new assertions and the hint that the questioner was himself a Communist tool.

By September of 1953 McCarthy had overstepped himself. He attacked the army, and his revelations were more than ever farfetched: a dentist commissioned in the army had belonged to a left-wing American Labor party; an army intelligence document entitled "Psychological and Cultural Traits of Soviet Siberia" was actually procommunist propaganda. Like most of his investigations, the army hearings were bitter, tasteless, and inconclusive, and McCarthy was running out of novelty. A courageous minority of senators finally brought a motion to censure him, in such terms that it was not so much a vote of confidence for or against McCarthy as for or against the Senate itself. The motion carried, and though McCarthy was subject to nothing but this verbal punishment, the aura of power, embattled rectitude, even invincibility that had surrounded him burst like a soap bubble. Within three years he died, a broken man, and it was then said of him that he was a "loud-mouthed kid who had elbowed his way to obscurity."

McCarthy is gone, but his meteoric rise and fall have left shame and a warning. The shame is not so much his as that of a government and a people that could be enthralled by his years of witch-hunting. The warning is the possibility of what might have happened had the United States at this time been seized by a paralyzing depression or been humiliated by a military defeat such as was the case in the German Republic when Hitler came to power.

Neo-Fascism The McCarthy era, with its fears and hatreds, sanctioned a variety of fascistic organizations great and small, comic and sinister, most of which clamored for the role of super-patriot. There were the Soldiers of the Cross, led by ultra-rightist Kenneth Goff, whose theme was "The United Nations is as Jewish as Coney Island." More dangerous were Robert DePugh's Minutemen. With a variety of titles such as the National Elite Guards of Ardsley, Pennsylvania, and the Illinois Internal Security Force, they held seminars in guerrilla warfare and piled up weapons for the great resistance day. Related was the American National party with its magazine *Kill*. Such groups, especially the Patriotic party behind DePugh, felt that political action alone was insufficient to resist the Communist conspiracy. They regarded themselves as simply the political arm of a complete patriotic resistance movement, the Minutemen, which at another time and place might have been called Storm Troopers.

A 1954 Supreme Court decision striking down the old racial segregation doctrine of "separate but equal" had called for the integration of all public schools. This decision encouraged the rapid rebirth of the Ku Klux Klan, which had been officially disbanded in 1944. The Klan was reborn not as one clan, but as several. In Georgia, Eldon Edwards, a paint sprayer from Atlanta, led the Knights of the Ku Klux Klan, a group favoring moderate action. In Alabama, Asa Carter was more of an activist and his following believed in castrating Negros as part of the Klan initiation ceremonies. Not until 1963 did the White Knights of the Ku Klux Klan in Mississippi begin active recruitment under the leadership of Sam Bowers, a vending machine repairman. By then, the civil rights movement was officially labeled a Jewish-Communist conspiracy and it was presumed to operate from Washington with an army of blacks being trained in Cuba to invade Mississippi. The summer of 1964, when various civil rights groups had planned to encourage Negro voter registration in Mississippi, was seen as a time of final confrontation.

Mississippi, of course, had no territorial ambitions outside of its borders, which removed it from the category of true fascism. But the emotional climate of hate and suspicion and the

FASCISM

official conduct of the police and other state agencies brought on by the supposed Negro and Communist conspiracy varied little from Fascist Germany in 1936.

In 1962 the integration of "Ole Miss," the state university, by the addition of one Negro student had been greeted by riot, the burning of cars, the wounding of federal marshals, and the fatal shooting of a reporter. Now, two years later, the prospect of Negroes gaining the vote, representing as they did 42 percent of the population, set the Klan to loading its guns and preparing its fire bombs. One episode alone need be documented. In June several hundred civil rights workers, mostly white, mostly collegiate, were expected to "invade" the state for the purpose of registering the Negro vote. For this invasion Mississippi braced itself to fight back. Local police and fire departments were to be coordinated so that they could rush statewide to the scene of any riot. The Klan had a more final solution.

In Philadelphia, county seat of Neshoba County, it was led by a Baptist minister called "The Preacher." The preacher's target was Michael Henry Schwerner, known to the Klan as "Goatee." Schwerner was an outsider, a young Jew from New York, and he had been working in Mississippi for several months, preparing a center for the summer project. The Longdale Negro Methodist Church was a hoped-for center of civil rights activity. Before the congregation had even decided whether or not to cooperate with Schwerner, the church burned to the ground. No arsonists were arrested.

Schwerner, accompanied by James Chaney, a local black civil rights worker, and Andrew Goodman, just arrived for the summer project, went out to visit the ruin. Before they could return to Meridian, they were arrested for speeding. Chaney was the driver, but all three were held in the county jail until after dark and until the Klan conspirators could gather outside. That night the three civil rights workers vanished. Some Mississippians called it a trick. They were hiding out in Cuba to give the state a bad name. Weeks later, deep in a dirt dam on a farm called "the Old Jolly Place," the bullet-riddled bodies were found by the FBI. Subsequently arrests were made; all suspects were Klan-associated, several of them members of the police force. This was by no means surprising, for traditionally the police are paid by the establishment to maintain law and order and preserve the status quo. In times of particular social stress, it becomes natural for them to gravitate to the conservative Right. Despairing of the possibility that these upright southern citizens would be convicted of murder by a Mississippi state court, the only recourse was to try them under federal law. The charge was not murder, but interference with the victims' civil rights, a crime that carried only a light sentence.

These three civil rights workers were not the only ones to die that summer. The Longdale church was not the only one to go up in flames. Dozens of civil rights workers were imprisoned on trumped-up charges. Many of them were beaten without mercy. Almost all were threatened by a society fearing the mongrelization of its Anglo-Saxon blood as Germany had seen her Aryan ideal being destroyed by international Jewry. Still, these events, too, were far from fascism. Mississippi is but a state, subject, however much it proclaims states rights, to federal law. But it has an emotional climate in which fascism could flourish, and as a matter of fact, in 1964 that climate was not limited to the deep South or to the Klan. It tainted the Republican convention in San Francisco that summer, and the party's nominee, Barry Goldwater, refused to accept a platform amendment condemning the Klan and other extremists. Goldwater remarked that extremism in defense of liberty was no vice and moderation in pursuit of justice was no virtue. Later, in fact, he would reject Klan support, although he got its endorsement anyway, along with almost unanimous backing from Mississippi's white voters.

As Goldwater would reject the Klan, so eventually would most sophisticated conservatives, and its fragmented elements have not succeeded in developing a nationwide movement as in the 1920s. This coolness toward the Klan exists even in the

FASCISM

South, largely because of an alternative organization, the White Citizens Council, made up of "respectable" southerners. The first such council was born in the Mississippi Delta just after the Supreme Court decree against segregated schools. Keeping the Negro in his place by more civilized and sophisticated measures such as the boycotting of shops and the firing of employees was the prime order of the council's business, and within ten years membership grew in the South to one million, made up in part of ex-Kluxers but including many prosperous businessmen. In order for this bigotry to enjoy wider appeal and justification, the civil rights movement was linked to the world-wide Communist conspiracy. Gradually, the more respectable elements have withdrawn from the White Citizens Council, and the tendency today is for it to drift closer to the Klan in its thinking.

The most subtle and influential of recent far-right extremist groups is the John Birch Society, founded in 1958 by a retired candy-maker, Robert Welch. The society's name is in honor of a Baptist missionary who served behind the lines in China during World War II and who was allegedly killed by Chinese Communists ten days after the war was over. This made him the first American casualty of the cold war, according to the Birchites.

The Birch Society is disciplined and well-organized. Its headquarters is in San Marino, California, with other offices in Glenview, Illinois; White Plains, New York; and Washington, D.C. Four thousand grass-root chapters are scattered about the country. A magazine, *American Opinion,* whose goal is shaping Americanism, is published monthly. A line of children's books is available, beginning-to-read books and "Living American Stories." In its local cellular structure and its goal of establishing a dedicated minority, or vanguard, the Birch Society is more Communist than Fascist. In beliefs and objective, however, it is entirely right-wing, adhering to the theory that Washington has been taken over by Communists, that the State Department works to advance global Communist conquest, and that Americans, so long as they are led by their enemies, can anticipate only defeat. Given such a vision, the Birchers' objective is to enlighten a hoodwinked society and in the end to obtain political power.

Only in the means to be used has there been dissension, namely, whether to develop a distinct "third party" or to infiltrate existing major parties. In 1964 the Birchers actively promoted Barry Goldwater for President. Their third-party champion, Kent Courtney, has long headed the "Conservative Society of America" and, as early as 1960, sought Goldwater for the party's standard bearer. In 1965 it was flirting with George Wallace as a possible leader. By this time the world Communist conspiracy was causing less excitement than the civil rights issue, and the Birchers had noticeably shifted their ground to law and order and the suppression of Negro violence. These issues were so appropriate to the Wallace presidential campaign of 1968 that they worked wholeheartedly for his election.

While not campaigning in elections, the Conservative Society has actively urged breaking off diplomatic relations with Communist countries, withdrawal from the United Nations, liberating Cuba and Red China, ending civil rights legislation, and repeal of the income tax. Though anti-Semitism has never been part of the party line and has been actively disavowed by Welch himself, the Birch syndrome is such as naturally to attract anti-Semites into the fold.

The Birch Society cannot be condemned for slackness. Thanks to its great wealth, its activities are many and varied. The first order of business is recruitment, and peak membership has been established at about 100,000. The other major endeavors can be divided generally into opposition to communism and the obstruction of civil rights. In its wide attack on communism, the Birch Society opposes the income tax as a plot devised to turn the United States into a Marxist-style collective society. The United Nations, of course, is part of the great conspiracy, and toward withdrawal of the United States the Society has circulated such postcards as a photograph of the United Nations building entitled "The House that Hiss Built." (The reference is to Alger Hiss, a U.S. State Department official convicted of espionage in 1950.)

The John Birch Society, which, had its dreams been realized, would have achieved a state of neo-fascism, reached its zenith of popularity in the mid-1960s. At first it was favored by a number of conservatives, who later came to the conclusion that Welch was destroying the conservative movement. At the 1964 Republican convention, many members were swept into the society fold. More were acquired after Goldwater's defeat under the slogan "Now will you join the John Birch Society?" Nevertheless, stagnation was setting in, and such comments by Robert Welch as his allegation that President Eisenhower was a conscious agent of the Communist conspiracy simply couldn't be swallowed.

The United States has had and still has a generous assortment of superconservative neo-Fascist organizations. But at the moment none are strong and few are as strong as they were in the more fearful fifties and sixties. The Ku Klux Klan has been largely discredited. The John Birch Society has lost novelty. The panic fear of communism that has nurtured many of these far-rightist groups has subsided, and a strengthened conservative Republican party, as well as a small Conservative party, offer outlets for the political aspirations of all but a desperate fringe.

The Future of Fascism

Fascism remains a well-exercised term of abuse. It is directed liberally toward parents, politicians, political parties, and national governments. It has even been used of the Black Panthers of the Black Power Left, whose closed-fist salute is reminiscent of il Duce. All rebels sanction terror and violence, from Spartacus to Cromwell and his Roundheads, from John Brown to the Irish Republican Army, but the radical blacks favor no super-nation. They are, in fact, antimilitarist and antinationalist. They represent the class struggle that Hitler denounced. They regard the state as already too strong, whereas the Fascists found it never powerful enough. Their antisocial methods alone do not make them Fascist, any more than does a college professor's work on military-related projects, or a politician's predilection for big business. Rarely, in fact, is the term *fascism* accurately applied if it is to retain its classic attributes: namely, fear of communism, the development of a state-dominated capitalism, popular mass support for a dictatorial head of state, and chauvinism leading to a military buildup and finally territorial expansion.

Groups and individuals may sometimes adhere to these principles, but they are nowhere nationally dominant. In all governments, from Communist to capitalist, fascistic elements can be found. Some governments or countries, like Portugal, exemplify the more prosaic economic structuring promoted by fascism, the so-called corporate state. Others, like South Africa and the State of Mississippi, exemplify the hysterical racist climate that creates the enthusiasm required by fascism. Police states and dictatorships abound, as they always have and perhaps always will, but as such they are not Fascist.

What of the future? Has fascism any prospects? As long as there are wars, national patriotism, depressions, prejudice, charismatic leadership, there remains the possibility of fascism reoccurring. But politics, like everything else on this planet, evolves, and for now the Fascist era of 1919–1945 is over. It would seem at this moment to be an atavism happily left behind.

In Western Europe, where the system flourished, although neo-Fascist political elements are active in Germany and Italy, the parties have not won consistent support, and there is no revival of the semireligious frenzy of the 1920s. Today Europe's political atmosphere is sober, dull, and prosperous. It holds no serious Fascist threat. There is, however, always the possibility of another war with its subsequent inflation or a worldwide depression that could upset the social balance. Either eventuality, particularly if combined with a threat from the Left, could galvanize the conservative elements into some form of neo-fascism.

The United States is experiencing a relatively conservative era, and one where the doctrine of world Communist conspiracy has been dismissed or at least downgraded. It is not fertile Fascist ground, either, but the radical Right does not lack an issue. Today it is civil rights and the black man. Thrusting ahead energetically, he is making progress. He has his dedicated organizations and he has his hope for the future. Opposed and threatened is the white working-class man stuck at a certain income level in a tedious job without much prospect of improvement. He sees the black man coming on at his expense, and this, rather than communism, is likely to be the basis for rightist extremism of the future. Some have called it the "New American Dilemma," and such a dilemma is apt to simmer for a long time without overturning the society or the government. The danger, in the United States and elsewhere, is not from torch-light-parading Fascists of the old school, but from the apathy of well-meaning citizens. Complacent in their democracies, they are unmindful of the possible erosion of democratic habits by pre-Fascist and pro-Fascist attitudes.

Definitions

Afrikaner Generally a native white South African of Dutch extraction who speaks the Afrikaans language.

Alsace-Lorraine An area in northeastern France, the title to which has been disputed by Germany, and which was taken by that country in the Franco-Prussian War and again in World War II. The area is now part of France.

American Nationalist Party A front group organized by the American Nazis before World War II to attract a native following.

American Opinion The name of a magazine published by the John Birch Society for the purpose of influencing political thinking toward their far-right position.

Anschluss In German the word means "a bringing together," and in the capitalized form it refers to that episode in 1938 when Nazis in Germany and Austria successfully conspired to unite the two countries.

Arditi Italian shock troops made famous by their valor in World War I. Later, many drifted into the Fascist movement.

Arditi del Popolo Italian name for the People's Shock Troops. They were organized by the political Left after World War I to resist Mussolini's Blackshirts.

Arrow Cross   The name of a Hungarian pro-Fascist political organization of the 1930s.

Aryan   A hypothetical ethnic grouping of those descended from early Indo-European peoples, as used in Hitler's racist theories.

Avanti   Title of an Italian Socialist newspaper for which Mussolini once worked. Fired for his diverging views, he thereafter made a point of persecuting the paper.

Authoritarianism   In political terms, refers to a governmental system in which individual freedom is subjected to state authority, this authority being held by one man or a small group of men over whom the people have no control.

Axis   The line about which a rotating body revolves. Adopted by Mussolini to describe the Fascist alliance of Italy, Germany, and Japan.

Black Panthers   An extremist American Black political group formed in 1966 with encouragement from Stokely Carmichael.

Blackshirts   The term referred first to Mussolini's Fascist militia, later to Hitler's bodyguards—the Nazi Schutzstaffel (SS)—because both groups wore black shirts as part of their uniform.

Broederbond   In South Africa, an elite clique of Afrikaners devoted to controlling the government in their own interest.

Brownshirts   Hitler's civilian army, also called Storm Troopers.

Camelots du Roi   Before World War I, the extreme patriotic Right in France established this organization along paramilitary lines. It was a prototype for the Blackshirts and Storm Troopers to follow.

Cartel   An international trust or business combination designed to fix prices on certain products.

Chauvinism   From Nicolas Chauvin, a Napoleonic soldier of excessive patriotism; the word means excessive promotion of national interests.

Christian Social Workers' Party   An anti-Semitic political party made up of workers, formed in Germany in 1879.

Concentration Camp   The term for those centers established under the Nazis to confine political and ethnic "undesirables." Although thousands died in these camps, generally from neglect, malnutrition, and disease, they are to be distinguished from the later extermination camps, which were not punitive in intent but designed for the liquidation of Jews, Communists, and others.

Corporate State, The   The objective of Italian fascism; the organization of the national economy as one big governmental corporation.

Danzig Now a Polish city, formerly a self-governing free seaport. Desired by Germany in 1939, its possession was one of Hitler's excuses for attacking Poland.

Dictatorship Government run by one man, a dictator, having absolute power.

Doctrine of Fascism Title of a book by Mussolini published in 1932, it was an attempt to give a philosophical structure to his already achieved seizure of power.

Dreyfusards The supporters of Alfred Dreyfus, a French Jewish army officer accused and convicted of treason on dubious evidence. His conviction was later set aside.

Duce, Il In Italian, "the Leader." Adopted by Benito Mussolini as his title as ruler of Italy.

Falange Spain's Fascist party, founded in 1933. The name *Falange* comes from the Spanish word for phalanx, a body of close-ranked troops.

Fasci di Combattimento A hard core of fighting Fascists set up by Mussolini just after World War I to combat the spread of communism in northern Italy.

Fortress Economy An economy believed to be self-sufficient within national boundaries and therefore better able to support a war effort.

Führer German word for "Leader," adopted by Adolf Hitler as his title as ruler of Germany.

German-American Bund American extension of the German Nazi party in the 1930s.

Gestapo Geheime Staatzpolizei, Nazi secret police.

Hitler Youth A Nazi youth organization created early in the movement and virtually compulsory for German young people just before World War II. Devoted to a quasi-military athletic program and the absorption by the members of Nazi dogma.

Imperial Fascist League A small group of Fascists in Britain before World War II who emulated nazism.

Invisible Empire Another name for the Ku Klux Klan.

Irish Republican Army Known as the IRA, a militant group seeking the independence of Northern Ireland (Ulster) from Great Britain.

Iron Guard Garda de Fier, a Rumanian group founded in 1930 to resist Jewish communism; basically Fascist.

John Birch Society Formed in 1958, this conservative American political group has directed its efforts to combating the supposed Communist conspiracy to take over the United States.

Junker The aristocratic landowners of East Prussia. They have long supported the German military tradition.

Keynesian Economics Refers to the economic theories of John Maynard Keynes (1883–1946), which holds, among other points, that varying interest and tax rates and public expenditures will control inflation.

Lapua Movement A group in Finland, gaining strength in the early 1930s, that favored a crushing of the Communist party and the development of a more Fascist government.

League of Patriots A pre-Fascist group in France that blamed the nation's shortcomings, particularly the failure to construct the Panama Canal, upon international Jewish finance.

Legion of Archangel Michael An elite group of Rumanian romantics who imagined themselves as knights-errant crusading against international Jewry in the 1920s.

McCarran Internal Security Act An act passed by the United States Congress during the Red scare of the 1950s to require registration by members of the Communist party.

Mein Kampf Adolf Hitler's autobiography, which set forth his political theories and his plans for conquest.

Mercantilism Traditionally a state economic policy of hoarding precious metals, particularly gold, and by massive exports establishing a favorable balance of trade.

Minutemen Those who were ready on a moment's notice to resist the British in the early days of the American Revolution; the name has been adopted by a right-wing American group armed against Communist attack.

National Purity Party A Japanese group of young army officers in the early 1930s, devoted to old military virtues and the purging of Western liberalism.

National Union Salazar's name for a pressure group intended to move Portugal toward his version of a corporate state.

National Socialism The term applied to the political theory behind Hitler's Nazi party. In general it implied dictatorship and military expansion.

Nationalist Party   In South Africa, that political party made up primarily of white Afrikaners devoted to white supremacy.

Ordnungs Dienst   A Storm Trooper–type organization established in the United States in the 1930s by the German-American Bund.

Party of Racial Defense   A party established in 1923 by anti-Semitic Hungarian nationalists.

PIDE (Policia Internacional e de Defesa do Estado)   Portuguese police force given wide powers and accustomed to using brutal methods. Under Salazar it was compared to Hitler's Gestapo.

Polish Corridor   A strip of land given to Poland after World War I to give her access to the sea. As this separated Germany from East Prussia it was much resented by Germans, a feeling exploited by Hitler.

Popolo, Il   Socialist newspaper in Italy, which employed the then-Socialist Mussolini before World War I.

Reichstag   During the Weimar Republic in Germany, the lower house of Parliament. The building in which it was housed was called by the same name.

Requetes   In Spain, those who supported the return of the king, Don Carlos, or his successor, to the throne.

Rhineland   That part of Germany west of the Rhine River. As a buffer zone, it was demilitarized after World War I.

Roehm Purge   Ernst Roehm was the head of Hitler's Storm Troopers. Fearing that he sought power for himself, Hitler had Roehm and many of his group murdered in 1934.

Ruiterjag   A youth group formed in South Africa in the 1930s in partial imitation of the Hitler Youth.

Shirtless Ones   In Argentina, Perón's militant brawling workers' group, his storm troopers.

Smith Act   A 1940 act of the United States Congress that made not only an act of revolution but the advocacy of such an act itself a criminal offense.

Social Justice   A Nazi party magazine circulated in the United States before World War II.

State Capitalism   The term has been loosely applied to governments that dominate their business community.

Storm Troopers   A paramilitary organization set up by the Nazi party. Called officially the *Sturmabteilung* in German, it was also referred to as the SA and the Brownshirts.

Sudetenland   A part of Czechoslovakia that contained many Germans; on this excuse it was annexed by Germany in 1938, followed by the rest of Czechoslovakia.

Syndicalism   A movement whereby a federated body of industrial workers would come to dominate the means of production.

TACT (Truth About Civil Turmoil)   An American John Birch Society group with the purpose of showing that civil rights unrest was part of the greater Communist conspiracy.

Third Reich   Hitler's title for his new Germany. The First Reich was the Holy Roman Empire. The Second Reich was the empire established by Bismarck in 1871.

Totalitarianism   Government by one person or a small group holding absolute—total—control of the people and suppressing individualism.

United Officers Group (Grupo de Oficiales Unidos)   Name of the officers' clique that seized power in Argentina in 1943.

Versailles Peace Treaty   This treaty followed World War I, and the harsh conditions it imposed upon Germany were among the causes leading to World War II.

Vlaamsch National Verbond   This anti-Semitic, anti-capitalist political group was formed in Belgium in 1933.

Volk   In German, literally, "the people." The term was emphasized as signifying the unity of the Nazi community.

Voortrekkers   Originally, a group of Boer pioneers; later, name was taken by South African youth organization that developed in the 1930s along Hitler Youth lines.

Walloon   The French-speaking people inhabiting Belgium along the French border, and therefore somewhat French in outlook.

Weimar Republic   The German republic founded at the end of the First World War at the city of Weimar. It began in 1919 and was ended by the Nazis in 1933.

Yellow Shirts   A band of Czarist street toughs that vanished from Russia with the Communist revolution. They resembled the later German Storm Troopers.

Biographies

Alfonso XIII, León Fernando María Isidro Pascual Antonio (1886–1941): Last of a long line of Spanish monarchs, Alfonso XIII was forced to abdicate in 1931 after a period of domestic strife and died ten years later in exile.

Bismarck (in full: Bismarck-Schönhausen) Otto Eduard Leopold von (1815–98): Chancellor of the new German Empire. Advocated a stern foreign policy of "blood and iron," a motto later inscribed on the daggers of the Hitler Youth. His domestic policies were advanced in social areas.

Bötticher, Paul Anton (1827–91): A professor at Göttingen University. He translated many ancient texts into German and also advanced a political concept based on conquest of Russia and overthrow of an alleged Jewish conspiracy to dominate the world.

Brown, John (1800–59): Farmer and abolitionist, Brown was involved in the antislavery struggle that led to the nickname "Bloody Kansas" for that state. Later, trying to rally southern slaves, Brown seized the arsenal at Harpers Ferry. Defeated there, he was tried and hanged for treason.

Carmona, Antonio Oscar de Fragoso (1869–1951): Carmona rose to

power in Portugal in 1926, put down various uprisings, and, with
Salazar as prime minister, was repeatedly elected president, a
position he held until his death in 1951.

Carol II, king of Rumania (1893–1953): Married Princess Helen of
Greece, but went into exile three years later and divorced her.
Returned to his native Rumania, where he pushed his son from
the throne. In 1940 Hitler had him ousted and he fled, ultimately
to Mexico.

Ciano, di Cortellazzo, Galeazzo (1903–44): Ciano married Mussolini's
daughter Edda in 1930 and served il Duce in various diplomatic
positions. Never a convinced fascist, he was, despite his close-
ness to Mussolini, liquidated on Hitler's authority.

Corradini, Enrico (1865–1931): An Italian writer of plays and novels,
Corradini set up a nationalistic journal, Il Regno, denouncing
democratic government and urging imperialism. He was a forerunner of the establishment of Italian fascism.

Croly, Herbert (1869–1930): Born to literary parents, Croly founded
The New Republic and introduced an early form of "national socialism" in his influential book The Promise of American Life
(1909).

Cromwell, Oliver (1599–1658): Became the leader of the Parliament
side in the civil war against Charles I of England. Prevailed and
from 1653 ruled as "lord protector," an early example of the dictatorship of the common man.

Déroulède, Paul (1846–1914): Founder of the League of Patriots (La
Ligue des Patriotes). A French chauvinist and anti-Semite, he
brought a foretaste of fascism to France.

Dixon, Thomas (1864–1946): Baptist clergymen, his writings glamoriz-
ing the old Ku Klux Klan had much to do with its twentieth-cen-
tury revival.

Dollfuss, Engelbert (1892–1934): Chancellor of Austria who opposed
the Nazis with his own form of dictatorship. He was finally assassinated by the Nazis.

Dreyfus, Alfred (1859–1935): A French Army officer and a Jew, he
was tried and found guilty of treason against the French government. The conviction was questioned as prejudiced and based
on trumped-up evidence and Dreyfus was vindicated after serving five years on Devil's Island. The case remained a cause
célèbre for years after.

Forrest, Nathan Bedford (1821–1877): Lieutenant general in the Confederate army and early leader of the original Ku Klux Klan. He later repudiated the organization when its methods turned brutal.

Franco, Francisco (1892–   ): Spanish soldier, elevated to command and finally dictatorship during the Spanish civil war. He has ruled over Spain ever since.

Fritsch, Gustav Theodor (1838–1927): German anthropologist and naturalist, publisher of *Der Hammer* a magazine calling for racial purity.

Funk, Walther (1890–1960): German journalist, became head of the Nazi Press Bureau upon its creation in 1933. Later became minister of economics and head of the Reichsbank. After the war he was found guilty as a war criminal.

Geibel, Emanuel (1815–1884): A German poet whose chauvinistic writings gave inspiration to later Nazism.

Goebbels, Joseph Paul (1897–1945): An early supporter of Hitler, Goebbels rose to become Hitler's minister for propaganda. He and his family would remain loyal to the last. They committed suicide along with Hitler.

Goldwater, Barry (1909–   ): A conservative Republican senator and candidate for president in 1964.

Gömbös, Gyula (Julius) (1886–1936): A veteran of the First World War, Gömbös was an anti-Semitic racist. From 1932–36 he was premier of Hungary.

Hess, Rudolf (in full: Walter Richard Rudolf; 1894–   ): An early Nazi and close associate of Hitler, he occupied the rank of third importance in Germany. Distraught and deranged by the situation in Germany, Hess finally flew to Scotland, where he was made a prisoner of war. Later he was sentenced to life imprisonment as a war criminal.

Himmler, Heinrich (1900–1945): Schoolteacher, later head of the SS and the Gestapo and toward end of the war of the home front defense. When captured by the British he killed himself.

Hindenburg, Paul von (1847–1934): He took part in the Franco-Prussian War, was a hero of World War I, particularly in his victory over the Russians at Tannenberg in 1914. Later he was elected president. He defeated Hitler at the polls but appointed him chancellor shortly before his own death.

Hirohito (1901–   ): Hirohito has been the emperor of Japan since

1926. Revered as a god until the end of World War II, he now has the role of a royal figurehead.

Hitler, Adolf (1889–1945): Born in Austria, soldier in World War I, politician and early leader of the National Socialist German Workers' party, he rose to become dictator over Germany. World War II, which he initiated, lead to Germany's defeat and his suicide.

Kondyles, or Kondylis, Georgios (1879–1936): A soldier during World War I, Kondyles afterward took up Greek politics, overthrew the government, and set himself up as prime minister. Subsequently, in 1935, he helped put George II back on the throne.

Ley, Robert (1890–1945): Ley was the head of Hitler's labor department. Captured in 1945, he killed himself before he could be tried as a war criminal.

Long, Huey Pierce (1893–1935): Lawyer and later governor of Louisiana, a professed populist who used a number of fascist techniques. He became a U.S. senator in 1931 and was assassinated before he could run for president, which was his professed ambition.

Ludendorff, Erich Friedrich Wilhelm (1865–1937): A hero of World War I, Ludendorff gave early support to Hitler in 1923. For a time he remained Hitler's passionate supporter, then became repelled by him and developed into a pacifist.

Malan, Daniel (1874–1959): South African politician who encouraged racial policy of apartheid.

Matteotti, Giacomo (1885–1924): Italian Socialist, who, after speaking out against Mussolini, was murdered by Fascists.

Maurras, Charles (1868–1952): A prolific French writer who devoted himself to totalitarian ideas. A pre-Fascist, he later sympathized with the Nazis.

Metaxas, Joannes (1871–1941): Greek general and later dictator.

Mosley, Sir Oswald Ernald (1896–   ): English politician who drifted to the Right and finally founded the British Union of Fascists. The party collapsed with the coming of World War II.

Mussolini, Benito (1883–1945): An Italian Socialist, Mussolini moved toward the Right and finally founded the Italian Fascist party, with which he rose to power in 1922. As a junior partner in World War II, Mussolini was eclipsed by Hitler and ruled over his country as a German puppet after having been deposed by the Italian king. He was executed by Italian partisans.

Pangalos, Theodoros (1878–1952): Greek general who became dictator of Greece in 1925, president in 1926, and later that same year was deposed and jailed.

Perón, Juan Domingo (1896–   ): Colonel, later general in the Argentine Army. As secretary of labor he won the favor of the workingman and rose to the position of dictator, only to be overthrown by the military in 1955. After eighteen years of exile in Spain he returned to Argentina in 1973.

Perry, Matthew Calbraith (1794–1858): An officer in the U.S. Navy, he took part in breaking up the slave trade and commanded the fleet that went to Japan, where he obtained the first commercial treaty with that country in 1854.

Pétain, Henri Philippe (1856–1951): French hero of Verdun in World War I, he later during World War II cooperated with the Nazi invaders and ruled as premier of unoccupied France from 1940 to 1944. Finally tried as a war criminal, he was sentenced to death, but his sentence was then commuted, and he later died in prison.

Rivera y Orbaneja, Miguel Primo de (1870–1930): Overthrew the Spanish government in 1923 and became dictator. Not successful as premier, he was forced by the king to retire and died in exile.

Rivera, José Antonio Primo de (1890?–1936): Son of the above, he established the Falangist party in Spain; was captured by the republican forces and executed.

Rosas, Juan Manuel de (1793–1877): Though officially only the governor of Buenos Aires, Rosas ruled other Argentine provinces. A chauvinist, he waged war against Uruguay and Brazil, and this last venture lead to his defeat and exile in 1852.

Salazar, Antonio de Oliveira (1889–1970): Professor of economics and Portuguese prime minister and virtual dictator from 1936 until his final illness in 1968. Salazar advocated a corporate-type governmental and social system that has been compared to fascism in some of its aspects.

San Martín, José de (1778–1850): Argentine hero and, in 1817, liberator of that country from Spain. He also was responsible for the defeat of the Spanish in Chile and Peru.

Smith, Ian Douglas (1919–   ): Leader of white supremacists in Rhodesia.

Stalin, Joseph (Iosif Vissarionovich Dzhugashvili) (1879–1953):

Member of the Bolshevik party, later party secretary, and thereafter dictator of Soviet Russia until his death.

Stoecker, Adolf (1835–1909): German protestant clergyman who, as a violent anti-Semite, formed the Christian Social Workers' party. In 1890 he was dismissed as the Berlin court pastor for his political activities.

Strasser, Gregor (1892–1934): Member of the Nazi party who quarreled with Hitler over the proper direction of national socialism. The quarrel lead to his assassination in 1934.

Thyssen, Fritz (1873–1951): Industrialist and head of great German iron and steel empire. He supported Hitler initially, broke with him when Hitler entered a pact with Russia, fled to Switzerland, and ended the war in a concentration camp.

Tojo, Hideki (1885–1948): Rose through the Japanese military ranks to become prime minister in 1941. Deposed when the war began to go badly, he was executed thereafter as a war criminal.

Verwoerd, Hendrik F. (1901–1966): South African, prime minister and leader of the apartheid white supremacy campaign there during its formative years.

Victor Emmanuel III (1869–1947): King of Italy, he was forced to accept Mussolini as prime minister in 1922 but with military support was able to depose him in 1943.

Bibliography of Sources

Allen, William Sheridan. *The Nazi Seizure of Power.* Chicago: Quadrangle Books, 1965.

Arendt, Hannah. *The Origins of Totalitarianism.* New York: Harcourt, Brace and World, 1951.

Bernard, Jack F. *Up from Caesar . . . a Survey of the History of Italy from the Fall of the Roman Empire to the Collapse of Fascism.* New York: Doubleday, 1970.

Bullock, Alan. *Hitler: A Study in Tyranny.* New York: Harper, 1953.

Cantril, Hadley. *The Psychology of Social Movements.* New York: John Wiley and Sons, 1941.

Carlson, John Roy. *Under Cover: My Four Years in the Nazi Underworld of America.* New York: E. P. Dutton, 1943.

*Carsten, Francis Ludwig. *The Rise of Fascism.* Berkeley: University of California Press, 1967.

Chalmers, David M. *Hooded Americanism, The First Century of the Ku Klux Klan.* New York: Doubleday, 1965.

Deakin, F. W. *The Brutal Friendship.* New York: Harper, 1962.

*Ebenstein, William. *Today's Isms.* Englewood Cliffs: Prentice-Hall, 1954.

* These titles are among the most generally readable on the subject of fascism.

Epstein, Benjamin R., and Forster, Arnold. *The Radical Right.* New York: Random House, 1966.

———. *The John Birch Society.* New York: Random House, 1966.

Fernsworth, L. *Spain's Struggle for Freedom.* Boston: Beacon Press, 1957.

Galvão, Henrique. *Santa Maria: My Crusade for Portugal.* New York: World Publishing, 1961.

Gilbert, G. M. *The Psychology of Dictatorship.* New York: Ronald Press, 1950.

Giniewski, Paul. *The Two Faces of Apartheid.* Chicago: Henry Regnery Company, 1961.

Griffith, Ernest S. *Fascism in Action.* Washington, D.C.: U.S. Government Printing Office, 1947.

Griffith, Robert. *The Politics of Fear.* Lexington: The University Press of Kentucky, 1970.

Grunberger, Richard. *The Twelve Year Reich.* New York: Holt, Rinehart, 1971.

Hamill, Hugh M., Jr. *Dictatorship in Spanish America.* New York: Alfred A. Knopf, 1966.

Kahn, Ely J. *The Separated People.* New York: W. W. Norton, 1968.

Kay, Hugh. *Salazar and Modern Portugal.* New York: Hawthorn Books, 1970.

Legum, Collin, and Legum, Margaret. *South Africa, Crisis for the West.* New York: Praeger, 1964.

Lipset, Seymour M., and Raab, Earl. *The Politics of Unreason.* New York: Harper & Row, 1970.

Livermore, Harold V. *A New History of Portugal.* Cambridge, England: Cambridge University Press, 1967.

Lowe, David. *Ku Klux Klan: The Invisible Empire.* New York: Norton, 1967.

Madariaga, Salvador de. *Spain: A Modern History.* New York: Praeger, 1958.

Newberry, Mike. *The Yahoos.* New York: Marzani and Munsell, 1964.

Nolte, Ernst. *Three Faces of Fascism.* New York: Holt, Rinehart, 1966.

Noyes, Alfred. *If Judgment Comes.* New York: Frederick Stokes, 1941.

Pattee, Richard. *Portugal and the Portuguese World.* Milwaukee: Bruce Publishing, 1957.

Paul, Elliot. *The Life and Death of a Spanish Town.* New York: Random House, 1937.

Phillips, Norman. *The Tragedy of Apartheid.* New York: David McKay Company, 1960.

Schomp, Gerald. *Birchism Was My Business.* London: The Macmillan Company, 1970.

Sender, Ramón. *Counter Attack in Spain.* Boston: Houghton Mifflin, 1937.

Shirer, William L. *The Rise and Fall of the Third Reich.* New York: Simon and Schuster, 1959.

Silver, James W. *Mississippi, the Closed Society.* New York: Harcourt, Brace and World, 1963.

Souchere, Eléna de La. *An Explanation of Spain.* New York: Random House, 1964.

Speer, Albert. *Inside the Third Reich.* New York: Macmillan, 1970.

Swing, Raymond G. *Forerunners of American Fascism.* Freeport: Books for Libraries Press, 1935.

Wheaton, Eliot Barculo. *Prelude to Calamity; the Nazi Revolution 1933–35.* New York: Doubleday, 1968.

* Whitehead, Don. *Attack on Terror: The FBI Against the Ku Klux Klan in Mississippi.* New York: Funk and Wagnalls, 1970.

* Woolf, S. J., ed. *European Fascism.* New York: Random House, 1968.

Index

Koiso, Kuniaki, 53
Kondyles, General Georgios, 62, *122*
Konoye, Fumimaro, 53
Korean War, 100-101, 102
Ku Klux Klan (U.S.), 62, 90, 97-100, 104, 109
    and civil rights movement, 104-107
    vs. communism, 12-13
    Italian Fascists compared to, 28

Landowners, 15, 16, 58
    German, 42, 69 (*see also* Junkers)
    Italian, 27, 67-68
    Spanish, 55, 56, 74-79 passim
"Lapua Movement" (Finland), 60, *115*
Lateran Treaties (1929), 31, 43
Latin America
    military dictatorships in, 14, 83
        (*see also* Argentina)
    Spain and, 76
Leader (role of), 15
    Hitler as, 15, 40, 41, *115* (*see also* Hitler, Adolf)
    Mussolini as, 15, 28 (*see also* Mussolini, Benito)
    See also Dictatorship
League of Nations
    Hitler and, 46
    U.S. and, 94
"League of Patriots" (France), 20, *116*
Ledesma Ramos, Ramiro, 55-56
Leese, Arnold Spencer, 64
"Legion of the Archangel Michael" (Rumania), 62, *116*
Ley, Robert, 43, *122*
Liberal capitalism, corporate state vs., 30
Library books, burning of, 10-11, 12
Libre Parole, La (French journal), 20
Libya, Italy and, 22
Long, Huey "the Kingfish," 94-97, 99, *122*
Longdale Negro Methodist Church

(Philadelphia, Miss.), 105, 106
Lossow, General Otto Von, 38
Loyalty oaths, 7, 42
Ludendorff, Erich Friedrich Wilhelm, 38, *122*
Luther, Martin, 40
Lutheran Church (Germany), 43

MacArthur, General Douglas, 4
McCarran Internal Security Act (U.S.), 102, *116*
McCarthy, Senator Joseph, 100-103
Malan, Prime Minister Daniel (South Africa), 88, *122*
Manchuria, Japan vs., 53
Mann, Thomas, 10
March on Rome (1922), 28-30, 37
Marx, Karl, 13
Matteotti, Giacomo, 29-30, *122*
Maurras, Charles, 21, *122*
Mediterranean Sea ("Mare Nostrum"), 31
Meiji Constitution (Japan), 51, 53
Mein Kampf (Hitler), 13, 38-39, 50, *116*
Mellon family (U.S.), 95
Melville, Herman, 10
Mercantilism, *116*
Metaxas, General Joannes, 60, 62, *122*
Middle Ages
    Jews in, 20, 23
    merchant guilds of, 67, 81
Militarism, 17
    Japanese, 52-54
    See also Military, The; War, glorification of
Military, The, 14, 16-17
    in Argentina, 83-84, 86
    in Austria, 59
    in France (*see* Dreyfus affair)
    in Germany, 42, 43, 75
    in Italy, 27-28, 75
    in Portugal, 81-82
    in Rumania, 62
    in Spain, 55, 56-57, 58, 74-79 passim (*see also* Spanish Civil War)

Index

About the Author

James D. Forman is a well-known author of books for young people, among them *Shield of Achilles, Ring the Judas Bell,* and *My Enemy, My Brother.* The last two titles were honored in the *Book World* Spring Book Festival in the year of their publication.

Mr. Forman is a graduate of Princeton University and Columbia University Law School. He has traveled widely in Europe, especially in Greece, a country that has served as background for a number of his books. Mr. Forman lives on Long Island.